HEGEL'S PHENOMENOLOGY
A PHILOSOPHICAL INTRODUCTION

PHILOSOPHY NOW

General Editor

ROY EDGLEY

*Professor of Philosophy
University of Sussex*

*

RICHARD NORMAN

Hegel's Phenomenology
A Philosophical Introduction

BENJAMIN GIBBS

Freedom and Liberation

Other Titles in Preparation

HEGEL'S PHENOMENOLOGY A PHILOSOPHICAL INTRODUCTION

RICHARD NORMAN
University of Kent

SUSSEX UNIVERSITY PRESS

1976

Published for
SUSSEX UNIVERSITY PRESS
by
Chatto & Windus Ltd
40 William IV Street
London WC2N 4DF

*

Clarke, Irwin & Co Ltd
Toronto

Hardback ISBN 0 85621 055 2

Paperback ISBN 0 85621 062 5

© Richard Norman 1976

Printed in Great Britain by
REDWOOD BURN LIMITED
Trowbridge & Esher

CONTENTS

Philosophy Now

English-speaking philosophy since the Second World War has been dominated by the method of linguistic analysis, the latest phase of the analytical movement started in the early years of the century. That method is defined by certain doctrines about the nature and scope both of philosophy and of the other subjects from which it distinguishes itself; and those doctrines reflect the fact that in this period philosophy and other intellectual activities have been increasingly monopolised by the universities, social institutions with a special role. Though expansive in number of practitioners, these activities have cultivated an expertise that in characteristic ways has narrowed their field of vision. As our twentieth-century ·world has staggered from crisis to crisis, English-speaking philosophy in particular has submissively dwindled into a humble academic specialism, on its own understanding isolated from substantive issues in other disciplines, from the practicial problems facing society, and from contemporary Continental thought.

The books in this series are united by nothing except discontent with this state of affairs. Convinced that the analytical movement has spent its momentum, its latest phase no doubt its last, the series seeks in one way or another to push philosophy out of its ivory tower.

ROY EDGLEY

Preface

This book is not a commentary on the *Phenomenology of Mind,* nor would I be competent to write one. What I have aimed at is a philosophical assessment of the *Phenomenology.* I have tried to identify what is of philosophical value in that work, and to examine and criticise Hegel's ideas. Naturally, since the book is intended for students and others who are reading the *Phenomenology* for the first time, I have had to give a good deal of attention to explaining what I take to be the meaning of Hegel's often obscure text. For the same reason I have thought it convenient to structure the book by following the sequence of Hegel's own sections, so that it can be read in conjunction with the *Phenomenology.* Nevertheless my basic aim has been to provide not an elucidation of Hegel, but a philosophical evaluation.

What one takes to be of philosophical value in Hegel depends upon one's own philosophical preoccupations, and I ought therefore to make mine explicit. In common with other contributors to this series, I write from a position of dissatisfaction with the dominant tradition in recent British philosophy. When I was first introduced to philosophy, as a student, analytical philosophy was the scarcely questioned orthodoxy. It carried with it its own conception of the history of philosophy, requiring one to leap from Hume, via Mill and Russell, to the analytical tradition, with perhaps a passing glance at Kant. Like others who have been dissatisfied with that orthodoxy, I believe that one way out of its constraints is to aim at an enlarged historical perspective. In reading Hegel, therefore, I am looking for a conception of philosophy more satisfactory than the analytical mode. The other main interest which I bring to the *Phenomenology* is an interest in Marx, together with a rejection of the academic divorce between such political interests and philosophical enquiry. Hegel provides an obvious point of contact between them. These preoccupations, then, will be apparent throughout the book.

I have not referred very frequently to other works on Hegel, but I could never have hoped to understand and learn from the

7

Phenomenology without the benefit of such works. I have profited a great deal from the writings of Kojève, Hyppolite, Marcuse, Loewenberg, Royce, Findlay, Baillie, Kaufmann and others.

I should like to thank Chris Cherry, Roy Edgley, Sean Sayers and Tony Skillen for their very helpful comments and criticism. I am also grateful to all the students with whom I have taken part in seminars on Hegel's *Phenomenology* over the last few years; I learned much from these discussions.

1

THE DILEMMA OF EPISTEMOLOGY

1. The *Phenomenology of Mind,* published in 1807, was Hegel's first major work, and was intended by him as an introduction to his whole philosophical system. As we shall see, Hegel took very seriously the problem of finding an appropriate starting-point for philosophy; and since the *Phenomenology* contains both a Preface and an Introduction, we might expect to find in these some account of what Hegel takes to be his starting-point and how he sees the *Phenomenology* as providing a way in to his philosophy.

In the case of the Preface, we should be disappointed. In it Hegel tries to do what he himself declares to be impossible, namely to explain the conclusion of the work in isolation from everything that leads up to it. I do not think that one can properly understand it until one has already read a good deal of the *Phenomenology.* The Introduction is another matter. It is genuinely introductory. In the first place, it is clearly written − clearer than much of the Preface. Moreover, it does not presuppose a knowledge of Hegel's philosophy. Rather, its main purpose is to relate the task of the *Phenomenology* to certain traditional conceptions of philosophy. I shall therefore devote this chapter to a detailed presentation and assessment of Hegel's Introduction.

2. The Introduction can be divided into three roughly equal sections (pp. 131^1-135^{12}, 135^{13}-139^4, and 139^5-145^{13}).[1] It begins as follows:

> 'It is natural to assume that before philosophy enters on its subject proper − namely, actual knowledge of reality − it must first come to an understanding of knowledge itself . . . . It seems legitimate to suppose, first, that there may be various kinds of knowledge, one of which may be better adapted than another for the attainment of our purpose . . . . and secondly, that since knowing is a faculty of a definite kind and with a determinate range, unless we determine its nature and limits more precisely we may take hold on clouds of error instead of the heaven of truth.' (p. 131)

This is a familiar idea. It represents the programme of epistemology in the traditional sense, the sense in which it was understood by Locke and Hume and Kant and has subsequently been understood by writers like Russell and Ayer. The suggestion is that, prior to the acquisition of knowledge, we have first to determine what may and what may not count as knowledge (e.g. the empiricist thesis would be that only knowledge-claims which can be verified by perceptual experience constitute genuine knowledge); that we have to identify the limits beyond which our knowledge cannot go; and that epistemology in this sense is necessary both as a preliminary to the rest of philosophy and in order to underpin the specialist sciences.

Hegel has particularly in mind the Kantian version of this approach. He refers to the idea of knowledge as 'an instrument by which we apprehend reality', or as 'a medium through which the light of truth reaches us', and recognizes that these ideas lead naturally to a particular form of scepticism. If knowledge is an instrument, actively applied to reality, it must alter what it is applied to, and consequently cannot give us things as they really are in themselves. Similarly, if knowledge is a medium through which reality is somehow filtered, then we can never know reality as it is in itself. Though Hegel makes no explicit reference to Kant, this type of scepticism is very recognisably Kantian. For Kant, knowledge is possible only insofar as experience is arranged in accordance with the forms of space and time and the categories. These are what we contribute, what we impose upon reality; therefore we can only know things within these forms, not things in themselves.[2]

Already, then, we can see hints of a programme for the *Phenomenology*: the overcoming of Kantian scepticism, the demonstration of the possibility of knowing things in themselves. But Hegel first rejects one way of carrying out such a programme. It might be supposed that one could get at things-in-themselves by identifying what knowledge, as instrument or as medium, contributes, and subtracting this so as to leave things-in-themselves as the result. I do not know whom Hegel has in mind here, although it would exactly describe (anachronistically) the philosophy of Schopenhauer, who supposes that since we contribute to experience the forms of space and time, reality itself must be outside space and time, and that since we organise experience into individual substances, reality itself must be one and indivisible. As Hegel says, however, reality is not to be caught, like a bird in a trap, by tricks of this sort. If we subtract from experience the way in which it has been shaped and organised by our knowledge, we are back where we started — prior to all knowledge (p. 132).

Hegel's own response to Kantian scepticism is to turn it upon itself. Such scepticism in fact involves a number of presuppositions: that knowledge *is* aptly characterised as an 'instrument' or a 'medium'; that there is a distinction to be made between 'knowledge' on the one hand and things-in-themselves or 'the Absolute' set over against it; and that this knowledge, cut off from the Absolute, can still appropriately be described as 'knowledge'. So, if we are indeed to be sceptical, why should we not refuse to accept these presuppositions — the very presuppositions which gave rise to scepticism in the first place? (pp. 132-3).

It may seem that Hegel is simply making an *ad hominem* point here. In fact, however, Hegel's argument strikes at the heart not just of Kantian epistemology but of the whole traditional conception of epistemology referred to at the beginning of the Introduction. The intention was that epistemology should be the starting-point, prior to all knowledge. But this is impossible. Any epistemological standpoint, against which all claims to knowledge are supposed to be tested, is *itself* a claim to knowledge. Hegel makes the same point, more clearly, later in the Introduction (p. 139): if we are to examine the various purported forms of knowledge, determining which of them are authentic, we seem to require some *criterion* of true knowledge; but at this stage, prior to the possession of knowledge, such a criterion or standard is precisely what we lack. Perhaps the clearest formulation of all, enlivened by a delightful analogy, is in the *Lesser Logic*:

> 'We ought, says Kant, to become acquainted with the instrument, before we undertake the work for which it is to be employed; for if the instrument be insufficient, all our trouble will be spent in vain . . . . Unless we wish to be deceived by words, it is easy to see what this amounts to. In the case of other instruments, we can try and criticise them in other ways than by setting about the special work for which they are destined. But the examination of knowledge can only be carried out by an act of knowledge. To examine this so-called instrument is the same thing as to know it. But to seek to know before we know is as absurd as the wise resolution of Scholasticus, not to venture into the water until he had learned to swim.' (*The Logic of Hegel* § 10)

Since I have suggested that this undermines not just Kant's philosophy but the whole enterprise of traditional epistemology, it may be as well to show how it applies to other philosophers besides Kant. Consider

11

Descartes's procedure in the *Meditations*. Having assured himself that he exists, and is a thinking thing, he goes on to say:

> 'In this first knowledge there is nothing that assures me of its truth, excepting the clear and distinct perception of that which I state, which would not indeed suffice to assure me that what I say is true, if it could ever happen that a thing which I conceived so clearly and distinctly could be false; and accordingly it seems to me that already I can establish as a general rule that all things which I perceive very clearly and very distinctly are true.' (*The Philosophical Works of Descartes* Vol. I, p. 158)

Obviously, this won't do. If Descartes knows that he exists and is a thinking thing on the grounds that he clearly and distinctly perceives it, then he is already *presupposing* that whatever he clearly and distinctly perceives is true, and so cannot thereby establish the principle. Therefore either the argument is circular, or there are prior grounds for asserting that whatever I clearly and distinctly perceive is true, in which case we are set upon an infinite regress.

The same dilemma arises for the empiricist principle that the only substantive knowledge consists in propositions which can be verified by perceptual experience. On what grounds is the empiricist principle itself known to be true? A classical empiricist such as Hume would claim that his theory of knowledge is, and can only be, itself established by an empirical study of human nature and the workings of the human mind. This is to commit the fallacy of circularity. More recent empiricists would adopt a different approach; logical positivists such as A. J. Ayer, for example, would if pressed assert that the Verification Principle cannot itself be empirically verified, nor is it what they would regard as the only other kind of meaningful proposition, a trivial tautology. But in that case, if it is supposed to convey genuine knowledge, as it surely must, then it is difficult to see how a vicious regress can be avoided.

I have cited these examples not just for their own sake but in order to show how Hegel's objection applies quite generally to epistemology as traditionally conceived. *Any* principle which specifies some criterion of what can and what cannot count as authentic knowledge must itself appeal either to that criterion (circularity) or to some other criterion (regress); and this is so because, as Hegel says, any such principle is itself a claim to knowledge. In view of its general applicability I shall refer to this dilemma as the Dilemma of Epistemology.

12

3. We might suppose that the only way to resolve this dilemma is to dispense with epistemological preliminaries altogether and go straight to the pursuit of positive knowledge. At first it seems that this is what Hegel advocates:

'With suchlike useless ideas and expressions about knowledge, as an instrument to take hold of the Absolute, or as a medium through which we have a glimpse of truth, and so on. . . , we need not concern ourselves . . . With better right, on the contrary, we might spare ourselves the trouble of taking any notice at all of such ideas and ways of talking which would have the effect of warding off science[3] altogether; for they make a mere empty show of knowledge which at once vanishes when science comes on the scene.' (pp. 133-4)

However, as the next paragraph indicates, Hegel does not in fact regard it as legitimate to embark on what one claims to be 'science' without any further justification. For, as he says, 'science, in the very fact that it comes on the scene, is itself a phenomenon' — that is to say, it is one particular claim to knowledge, which presents itself alongside other similar and competing claims. It presents itself as worthy of being adopted in preference to these rival claims. But why should it be adopted? To what does it appeal in order to justify itself? It cannot urge the rejection of other forms of knowledge simply on the grounds that these conflict with itself and are therefore false; for precisely the same justification could be urged on behalf of these other forms of knowledge, and 'one barren assurance is as good as another.'

Despite the rejection of tranditional epistemology, then, something akin to it, some kind of preliminary, is still needed. Science must first establish its credentials before it can claim to be the truth. And this preliminary investigation is to take the form of a phenomenological study:

'Science must liberate itself from this phenomenality, and it can only do so by turning against it . . . . For this reason we shall here undertake the exposition of knowledge as a phenomenon.' (p. 134-5)

Science must vindicate itself not by being measured against some preconceived criterion, but through a descriptive examination of its character as a specific phenomenon, from which its validity will emerge. This is what Hegel understands by a 'phenomenology'.

In the first of the three sections of the Introduction, then, Hegel has argued the need for a phenomenological preliminary to systematic knowledge, in place of the traditional epistemology. In the second section he will further elaborate what this 'phenomenology' is to consist in, and in the third section he will attempt to show how it provides a way out of the Dilemma of Epistemology.

4. The notion of a 'phenomenology' has been introduced as that of an 'exposition (which) has for its object only phenomenal knowledge' — that is to say, an exposition of knowledge as a *phenomenon,* as it actually *appears,* not insofar as it conforms to some preconceived model. This idea, that philosophy must find its starting-point within ordinary consciousness, bears an initial resemblance to two other philosophical movements. The first of these is the later phenomenological movement initiated by Husserl, where the underlying idea is that of philosophy as a direct description of consciousness prior to any theory or explanation in terms of which it is interpreted. The second possible comparison is with the later work of Wittgenstein, and particularly with Wittgenstein's insistence that standards of correctness must be located *within* established ways of proceeding. In his discussion of the notion of 'following a rule', for example, he shows that since any rule can be variously interpreted the correct interpretation of a rule cannot itself be ultimately grounded in a rule, and that therefore ultimately the only justification can be 'This just is how we do go on!' Hence Wittgenstein's assertion that the use of language presupposes agreement in judgements, and that the judgements which people actually make are in some way constitutive of what counts as a correct judgement.[4]

Common to the Hegelian, the Husserlian, and the Wittgensteinian conceptions of philosophy is the recognition that philosophy cannot stand outside ordinary consciousness or ordinary discourse and assess it by reference to some external standard. They all build upon the realisation that the starting-point of philosophy must be, in this sense, pre-theoretical. Both for the phenomenologists and for Wittgenstein this could be put by saying that philosophy cannot explain, it can only describe.[5] Hegel however would not say this. His phenomenology is not just descriptive. In considering the next section of the Introduction we shall now begin to see how his conception of philosophy differs from the other two.

In the first place Hegel regards his 'phenomenology' as an examination not of an amorphous 'common sense' or 'ordinary language', but of various specific forms of knowledge:

14

'. . . the exposition . . . can be regarded as the path of the soul which is traversing the series of its own forms of embodiment' (p. 135)

Moreover the progression through these different forms of knowledge is not simply a descriptive survey but is essentially a *critical* enterprise — 'this pathway has a *negative* significance'. Each form of knowledge will be shown to be inadequate, so that it cannot be regarded as true knowledge; and 'because of that, the road can be looked on as the path of doubt, or more properly a path of despair.'

Such a procedure, subjecting all forms of knowledge to criticism and rejection, has an obvious affinity to scepticism as traditionally understood. Hegel therefore clarifies its relation both to normal, everyday doubt and to that Cartesian doubt which is the basis of modern philosophical scepticism. Everyday doubt is not systematic; it is haphazard, 'a jostling against this or that supposed truth, the outcome of which is the disappearance of the doubt again in due course and a return to the former truth.' Cartesian doubt, by contrast, is indeed systematic; it is 'the resolve . . . not to deliver itself over to the thoughts of others on their mere authority, but to examine everything for itself, and only follow its own conviction, or, still better, to produce everything itself and hold only its own act for true.'[6] But the trouble with this sort of scepticism is that it is disingenuous. It purports to be a developmental process, moving through doubt to the truth, but in fact it has decided in advance where it wants to get to; the development is presented 'in the form of an intended purpose, . . . as having already taken place.' Consequently such doubt is not genuine. The Cartesian sceptic thinks it appropriate to doubt all beliefs insofar as they rest on an appeal to authority, but puts an end to this doubt by appealing to his own private conviction. He thus ends up holding the same beliefs as were formerly held on authority, and differing, as Hegel says, only in the degree of his conceit.

Hegel's criticism has, I think, considerable force. Descartes begins the *Meditations* by resolving to doubt the existence of the external world, the truths of mathematics, the existence of God, etc., but he does so because he has decided in advance that his purpose in doubting them is to find a way of justifying them. The goal itself is never affected by the doubt. The doubt, in fact, is not serious.

Hegel's scepticism differs, he claims, in being genuinely developmental. It is an educative process. Doubt is entertained not in order to be banished, but in order to point the way to a new and more satisfactory set of ideas. The sceptical doubts cast upon each form of knowledge give rise to a *new* form which *replaces* it.

'The series of shapes, which consciousness traverses on this road, is . . . the detailed history of the process of training and educating consciousness itself up to the level of science'. (p. 136)

But how, we might ask, shall we know when we have reached 'the level of science'? In order to meet this question, Hegel is led to make a further claim: that the developmental process is a *necessary* sequence.

'The completeness of the forms of unreal consciousness will be brought about precisely through the necessity of the advance and the necessity of their connection with one another.' (p. 137)

The claim that each stage of the *Phenomenology* follows necessarily from the previous stage is a notoriously obscure and contentious claim. What kind of necessity is Hegel talking about? Logical necessity? Is he suggesting that each stage in some sense *entails* the next? Or is the necessity chronological? Is the sequence intended as a historical sequence, and is Hegel espousing a form of historical determinism? We shall return to these questions.

It cannot be said that Hegel throws much light on the matter in the present paragraph. He offers to explain the notion of 'necessity' by reverting to the difference between his phenomenological method and traditional scepticism. The latter is purely negative — or at any rate regards itself as such. But in fact negation is never merely negative. It is always a negation *of* something, a *determinate* negation, and as such it always has a positive content. Therefore the subjection of a form of consciousness to negative criticism must, as a result, give rise to a new form of consciousness.

This idea of 'determinate negation' is of central importance for the *Phenomenology*. It is what makes it a developmental sequence, with each stage of the sequence giving rise to another. It is not, however, of much help in explaining why the sequence should be seen as a necessary one; and I do not think that we shall be able to clarify this notion of 'necessity' until we have looked at the examples offered us in the main body of the *Phenomenology*.

Hegel concludes this sketch of the phenomenological process by indicating the goal of the development.

'The terminus is at that point where knowledge is no longer compelled to go beyond itself, where it finds its own self, and the notion
corresponds to the object and the object to the notion.' (p. 137-8)

This is hardly a translucently clear description. We might begin to make
sense of it by fastening on the final phrase − the reference to a correspondence between notion and object. At the most obvious level we can
take this to mean that the development comes to an end when there is
no longer a gap between how things are and how we think they are.
This is intelligible, but also unexciting; stated in these terms, the aim
of the *Phenomenology* is not startlingly different from, though perhaps
more ambitious than, that of any philosophical or intellectual enterprise. However, Hegel's phrase also has other connotations.

The word which Baillie translates as 'notion' is *'Begriff'*. This would
more naturally and appropriately be translated as 'concept'.[7] One ad-
vantage of the term 'concept' is that it is to be found in the standard
translations of Kant. Kant has a good deal to say about 'concepts' in
the *Critique of Pure Reason,* but he is particularly concerned with a
certain class of concepts, those 'pure *a priori* concepts' such as 'substance' and 'causality' which he also calls 'categories'. This takes us
back to the beginning of Hegel's Introduction, for we saw there that
he identified a specifically Kantian form of scepticism and regarded
it as a challenge to be met. If the pure *a priori* concepts are imposed
by us on reality, then for Kant this entails that there is a fundamental
distinction between these concepts and the nature of 'things in themselves'. So Hegel's talk of a correspondence between concept and object would refer also to the closing of this Kantian gap. The aim of
the *Phenomenology* would be to reach a point where there is no longer
a contrast between the categories which are valid 'for us' and things as
they are 'in themselves'.

It is in this context, I think, that we can also understand what Hegel
means by 'that point where knowledge is no longer compelled to go
beyond itself, where it finds its own self.' I would interpret this too as
an essentially Kantian claim: Hegel accepts Kant's view that the pure
a priori concepts are the product of the intellect, so that in encounter-
ing them 'knowledge . . . finds its own self'; and if Kant's residual
'things-in-themselves' are eliminated, it will then be the case that
'knowledge is no longer compelled to go beyond itself.' In knowing
reality, the intellect knows itself, because it knows what it has itself
put there. However, I recognise that the sentence which we are at

17

present examining is a fragile basis on which to build such an interpretation; I shall try to give it further support as we progress through the text of the *Phenomenology*.

To sum up this section of the Introduction: Hegel has characterised the *Phenomenology* as a necessary development through a sequence of forms of consciousness. Each form is posited by the criticism of the previous one, and the goal of the process is absolute knowledge understood as a complete correspondence of concept and object.

5. In the final section of the Introduction Hegel returns to the Dilemma of Epistemology. The *Phenomenology* has been presented as a preliminary to science. Its task will be to vindicate the claim of Hegel's 'science' to be genuine knowledge. Such a task is similar to that of traditional epistemology, and Hegel must therefore show that the phenomenological method escapes the difficulties which he has previously presented as fatal to traditional epistemology. He states the problem thus:

> 'This exposition, viewed as a process of relating science to phenomenal knowledge, and as an investigation and test of the reality of knowledge, does not seem possible without some presupposition which is laid down as an ultimate criterion. For a test consists in applying an accepted criterion, and, on the basis of an agreement or disagreement between it and what is tested, deciding whether the latter is right or wrong; and the criterion in general, and so also science if this is the criterion, is thereby accepted as the essence or as the in-itself. But here, where science first appears on the scene, neither science nor any sort of criterion has justified itself as the essence or as the in-itself, and without this no test seems possible.' (p. 139)

This is clearly the point at which the Dilemma of Epistemology presents itself. Hegel's answer to it is to be found in the suggestion that phenomenology employs an *internal* criterion; and this idea he now proceeds to elucidate.

He first states the problem in more formal terms. Knowledge presents itself as involving a distinction between *being-for-consciousness* and *being-in-itself*, i.e. between reality as we *know* it, on the one hand, and *truth* on the other. To put it more simply, knowledge is knowledge *of* something, of an object which is distinct from the knowledge itself. As Hegel adds, this is how the matter appears to the ordinary consciousness; how valid these distinctions are remains to be seen.

18

The problem can now be re-stated as follows (p. 140[6]). Given this dichotomy between being-for-consciousness and being-in-itself, we seem to be necessarily confined to one side of the dichotomy. We can only know things as they are for us, and therefore, conversely, we cannot know things as they are in themselves. Accordingly, in the present case, where we are investigating the nature of knowledge, we can only know what knowledge is for us, not what it is in itself. The criterion which we apply to it is *our* criterion, one which we have to presuppose, and there can be no independent way of knowing whether it is an objectively correct one.

Hegel now offers his solution (p. 140[18]). In the present case the object of our enquiry is itself *knowledge, consciousness.* The *Phenomenology* is an attempt to acquire knowledge of knowledge. Therefore the above dichotomy falls *within* the object of our enquiry, and we are *not* in this case confined to one side of the dichotomy. Given the subject/object dichotomy, what consciousness itself declares to be its object constitutes the criterion by which that consciousness is to be tested. Therefore we do not need to bring our criterion with us, as an external standard which is already presupposed. Consciousness itself supplies its own criterion.

This is rather cryptic. Let us supply an example. Consider the chairs and tables beloved of philosophers. Take first the case of my awareness of the table. The problem here is that I can know only the table as it appears to me. I can never compare my awareness of it with the table itself. This is what gives rise to epistemological scepticism. But now suppose that the object which I am considering is not *the table,* but *my knowledge of the table,* viewed as a certain general kind of consciousness. Suppose for example that I regard it as an example of the first kind of knowledge which Hegel considers in the *Phenomenology*: Sense-certainty. The characterisation of this knowledge-relation will involve *both* the characterisation of a certain kind of object *and* the characterisation of a certain kind of consciousness. In this case the form of consciousness is described as 'sense-certainty' and its objects are described as immediate sensory particulars, the particulars referred to by such terms as 'this', 'here', and 'now'. 'Thus' says Hegel,

> 'in what consciousness within itself declares to be the "in-itself" or the "true", we have the criterion which it itself sets up, and by which we are to measure its knowledge.' (p. 140).

In other words, we have to ask: if the objects of consciousness are

19

immediate sensory particulars, *is* sense-certainty in fact the kind of knowledge which one can have of such an object? The answer, as we shall see, will be: No. If the object is characterised simply in this way, then it cannot be an object of certainty at all. Consequently consciousness has to be redescribed, and sense-certainty has to give way to a *different* kind of knowledge.

> 'Should both, when thus compared, not correspond, consciousness seems bound to alter its knowledge, in order to make it fit the object. But in the alteration of the knowledge, the object itself also, in point of fact, is altered.' (p. 142)

The new characterisation of knowledge carries with it a new characterisation of the object. Sense-certainty, because it is inadequate to its object, gives way to the attitude of Perception. But this form of consciousness has its own proper object; it is a consciousness not of particulars but of universals – things and their properties – and so in this new object we now have a new criterion by which to judge the new form of consciousness.

Has Hegel then solved his initial problem? Whether the procedure he sketches here is a feasible one can be determined only by looking at its application to specific examples. But it does appear to meet his general demand. The criterion it employs to assess forms of consciousness is an *internal* criterion. This is crucial. It enables Hegel to escape from the Dilemma of Epistemology. It enables him to claim that, by employing the phenomenological method in place of traditional epistemology, he can avoid having to presuppose the validity of some external criterion. Simply by remaining within a form of consciousness, and describing it from within, he can assess it and criticise it. And he can do so because the internal description involves both a description of the object and a description of the knowledge, and the one can be tested against the other.[8]

For Hegel, the idea of an internal critique means not only that we do not have to supply an external criterion, but that we do not even have to do the testing.

> 'Not only in this respect, that concept and object, the criterion and what is to be tested, are ready to hand in consciousness itself, is any addition of ours superfluous, but we are also spared the trouble of comparing these two and of making an examination in the strict sense of the term; so that in this respect, too, since consciousness

tests and examines itself, all we are left to do is simply and solely to look on.' (p. 141)

This idea, that consciousness tests itself and that we have only to look on, is an odd-sounding one, but Hegel takes it very seriously. It determines the whole presentation of the *Phenomenology,* and accounts for some of its most disconcerting features. The work is written as a sort of 'biography' of Consciousness, a narrative account of the various experiences which Consciousness undergoes. Where other philosophers (the Empiricists, or Kant, or contemporary British philosophers) tend to speak of what *we* say, what *we* know, what *we* experience, Hegel talks of what *consciousness* experiences or recognises or discovers. Alternatively, some particular embodiment of consciousness is taken as the subject of experience – e.g. 'Sense-certainty wants to deal with the 'This'. Perception, on the other hand, takes what exists for it to be a universal' (p. 162). There are indeed passages where Hegel speaks of what *we* know to be the case; but these are always parenthetical, and are to be sharply distinguished from the main narrative. The implication is always: 'We, from our superior vantage-point as philosophers, know that such-and-such is the case, but consciousness itself does not yet realise this.'

This mode of presentation makes it very difficult to know just what status to attach to Hegel's assertions. In effect, there are no philosophical arguments of an orthodox sort. Consider the passage which we have just quoted:

'Sense-certainty wants to deal with the 'This'. Perception, on the other hand, takes what exists for it to be a universal.' (p. 162)

Does this mean: 'Some philosophers think that the objects of experience are particulars, other philosophers think they are universals'? Or does it mean: 'Human beings in general, when they have an immediate sensory awareness of something, think that they are dealing with a pure 'This"? Again, how are we to understand the criticism of such a position? Is it to be understood as the criticism of a philosophical theory, or of the assumptions involved in a form of everyday experience? Does it mean that people are *not* in fact certain of the immediate objects of sensory experience? or that they *ought* not to be? or that, though they are, this does not have the implications which philosophers have taken it to have? We have furnished ourselves with yet another set of questions which we shall have to bear in mind when reading the text.

Hegel's suggestion that consciousness does all the work, and that we have only to look on, is subsequently qualified (pp. 143-4). For it is we, the philosophical onlookers, who order the work of criticism into a continuous process of development. Consciousness stands in judgment on itself, but it is we who find in this criticism a new object for consciousness and thereby supply the next stage in the process of development. Reverting to the vocabulary of 'determinate negation', one could say that it is we who recognise that the negation is determinate, and who make explicit the positive implications of the negative criticism.

The final sentence of the Introduction reads:

> 'In pressing forward to its true form of existence, consciousness will come to a point at which it lays aside its semblance of being hampered with what is alien to it, with what is only *for* it and exists as an other, [it will reach a point] where appearance becomes identified with essence, where in consequence its exposition coincides with this very same point in the science proper of mind, and finally, when it grasps this its own essence, it will denote the nature of absolute knowledge itself.' (p. 145)

I take this to be simply a reiteration that the final goal of the *Phenomenology* is the point at which there is no longer a gap between knowledge and alien things-in-themselves.[9]

6. I have presented and analysed Hegel's Introduction in some detail. I take this degree of detail to be justified, first, because it *is* an Introduction. A number of crucial ideas are introduced here, and we need to set them out clearly if we are to understand what is going on in the main body of the work. But, secondly, I think it worth devoting a good deal of attention to the Introduction because it presents in a general form certain ideas which I take to be among the most valuable in the *Phenomenology*. These can be summarised in two basic points.

(i) The negative point first. The difficulty which Hegel sees as arising for traditional epistemology, and which I have referred to as the Dilemma of Epistemology, does seem to me to be an inescapable difficulty for that mode of philosophy. Any version of epistemology as traditionally conceived involves the fallacy of supposing that one can know before one knows.

(ii) Hence the positive point. Hegel's notion of a 'phenomenology', and of an 'internal critique', does seem to me to be the only viable alternative to traditional epistemology. The details of Hegel's method may be debatable. But he is surely right in this, that any adequate

STRUCTURE OF THE PHENOMENOLOGY OF MIND

A. CONSCIOUSNESS	I. Sense-certainty, the 'This' and Meaning		
	II. Perception, the Thing and Deceptiveness		
	III. Force and Understanding, Appearance and the Supersensible World.		
B. SELF-CONSCIOUSNESS	IV. The Truth of Self-certainty		
	IV.A. Independence and Dependence of Self-consciousness; Master and Slave		
	IV.B. Freedom of Self-consciousness; Stoicism, Scepticism, and the Unhappy Consciousness		
C.(AA) REASON	V.A. Observational Reason	a. Observation of Nature	
		b. Observation of Self-consciousness	
		c. Physiognomy and Phrenology	
	V.B Self-realization of Rational Self-consciousness	a. Pleasure and Necessity	
		b. The Law of the Heart and Fanaticism	
		c. Virtue and the Way of the World	
	V.C Individuality which takes itself to be real in and for itself	a. The Herd, Deception, and 'the Real Fact'	
		b. Reason as Legislator	
		c. Reason as Testing Laws	
(BB.) SPIRIT	VI.A Objective Spirit: Ethics	a. The Ethical World: Human and Divine Law, Man and Woman	
		b. Ethical Action: Human and Divine Knowledge, Guilt and Destiny	
		c. Legal Status	
	VI.B Self-estranged Spirit	I. The World of Self-estranged Spirit	a. Culture and the Real World
			b. Faith and Pure Insight
		II. Enlightenment	a. The struggle with superstition
			b. The truth of enlightenment
		III. Absolute Freedom and the Terror	
	VI.C Spirit certain of itself: Morality	a. The Moral World-view	
		b. Dissemblance	
		c. Conscience; the Beautiful Soul; Evil and Forgiveness	
(CC.) RELIGION	VII.A Natural Religion	a. God as Light	
		b. Plants and Animals as Religious Objects	
		c. The Artificer	
	VII.B The Religion of Art	a. The Abstract Work of Art	
		b. The Living Work of Art	
		c. The Spiritual Work of Art	
	VII.C Revealed Religion		

(DD.)
ABSOLUTE KNOWLEDGE

theory of knowledge must begin from within existing claims to knowledge, rather than from some externally presupposed criterion.

7. I shall end this chapter with some remarks on the structure of the *Phenomenology*. Hegel regards himself as precluded from setting this out in advance, because he sees it as emerging from the activity of consciousness, not externally imposed. This has led some writers to play down the existence of any systematic structure to the work. Nevertheless, it does have a clear formal structure, and an understanding of it can help us to get our bearings. At this stage I shall have to set it out dogmatically and let the justification emerge as we proceed through the book. I shall do so by reference to the accompanying diagram.

We have seen that the *Phenomenology* is a sequence of different forms of consciousness, each of which is subjected to criticism and thereby gives rise to its successor. These individual stages go all the way down the right-hand side of the diagram, progressing from Sense-certainty to Absolute Knowledge. They fall into six main sections, which are to be found in the left-hand column and can in turn be split into two groups of three. 'Consciousness', 'Self-consciousness' and 'Reason' are the basic divisions of *individual* experience, and 'Spirit', 'Religion' and 'Absolute Knowledge' are the basic divisions of *social* experience. In fact, 'Spirit', 'Religion' and 'Absolute Knowledge' are the social equivalents of 'Consciousness', 'Self-consciousness' and 'Reason', religion being the means by which a society attains to self-consciousness and expresses to itself its own nature.

The relation between the 'individual' and 'social' sections reflects the fact that, for Hegel, the individual is an abstraction from society. The individual cannot exist in isolation. Accordingly the first three main sections are abstractions from Spirit, and the modes of consciousness depicted therein can exist only within a determinate form of social life.[10] The advance from Consciousness to Self-consciousness, to Reason, and then to Spirit is therefore not a chronological sequence but a purely logical development, since these sections can themselves be separated only by philosophical analysis and abstraction. According to Hegel the sequence of stages *within* each of these major sections *is* a chronological development.[11] Nevertheless historical development proper begins only in the second half of the *Phenomenology,* with the progression from one stage of society to the next. 'Spirit' is in effect Hegel's recapitulation of human history. 'Religion' repeats the historical process at the level of the consciousness which each society has of itself. Absolute Knowledge is therefore the culmination not only of an intellectual development but also of human history.

It will be apparent that the sections and sub-sections of the work regularly fall into groups of three. It has sometimes been thought that this triadic structure constitutes the 'dialectical' character of Hegel's philosophy. The dialectic, it has been said, resides in the arrangement of 'thesis', 'antithesis' and 'synthesis' making up each triad. Recent writers have criticized this interpretation. J.N. Findlay points out that 'the terms 'thesis', 'antithesis' and 'synthesis', so often used in expositions of Hegel's doctrine, are in fact not frequently used by Hegel.'[12] Walter Kaufmann goes much further than this. He says, for example, that Hegel

'. . . never once used these three terms together to designate three stages in an argument or account in any of his books . . . . Whoever looks for the stereotype of the allegedly Hegelian dialectic in Hegel's *Phenomenology* will not find it. What one does find . . . is a very decided preference for triadic arrangements . . . . But these many triads are not presented or deduced by Hegel as so many theses, antitheses, and syntheses. It is not by means of any dialectic of that sort that his thought moves up the ladder to absolute knowledge' (W. Kaufmann, *op. cit.*, p. 168).

And in a footnote, he adds:

'The only place where Hegel uses the three terms together occurs in the lectures on the history of philosophy, on the last page but one of the section on Kant – where Hegel roundly reproaches Kant for having "Everywhere posited thesis, antithesis, synthesis" '. (*Op.cit.*, p. 168n)

Kaufmann has over-reacted. If we follow up his reference to the *History of Philosophy*, we find that what Hegel actually says is this:

'But besides the general idea of synthetic judgments *a priori* . . . , Kant's instinct carried this out in accordance with the scheme of triplicity, unspiritual though that was, in the whole system into which for him the universe was divided . . . Kant has therefore set forth as a universal scheme the rhythm of knowledge, of scientific movement; and has exhibited on all sides thesis, antithesis and synthesis, modes of the mind by means of which it is mind, as thus consciously distinguishing itself. The first is existence, but in the form of Other-

Being for consciousness; for what is only existence is object. The second is Being-for-self, . . . for self-consciousness, as the negative of Being-in-itself, is itself reality. The third is the unity of the two, . . . into which are re-absorbed both the objective and the independently existent subjective. Kant has thus made an historical statement of the moments of the whole, and has correctly determined and distinguished them: it is a good introduction to Philosophy.' (*History of Philosophy,* Vol. III, p. 477f.)

If this is how Hegel 'reproaches', his praise must be lavish indeed! Earlier in his discussion of Kant, we find him offering a similar assessment:

'It betrays a great instinct for the Notion when Kant says that the first category is positive, the second the negative of the first, the third the synthesis. The triplicity, this ancient form of the Pythagoreans, Neo-Platonists and of the Christian religion, although it here reappears as a quite external schema only, conceals within itself the absolute form, the Notion.' (*Ibid.,* p. 439. Cf. *Phenomenology of Mind,* pp. 107-8.)

So Hegel does indeed criticise Kant; in his concern to arrange all the categories in groups of three, Kant fails to penetrate to the basic conceptual relations which underlie this arrangement. Nevertheless, he has stumbled intuitively upon the appropriate external form of those relations. Similarly the triads in the *Phenomenology* are important not as a mechanical schema but because of the movement of thought which they express. Hegel is not obsessed by triads, but he *is* 'obsessed' by the problem of *opposites* and of their reconciliation. More specifically, as can be seen from the passage on Kant and from our earlier analysis of the Introduction, he is preoccupied with the opposition of *subject* and *object.* Closely connected with this is the opposition of *particular* and *universal* – for, like Kant, Hegel links objectivity with universality. These pairs of opposites determine the structure of the *Phenomenology.* In the triad Consciousness/Self-consciousness/Reason, for example, Consciousness isolates the aspect of the object, Self-consciousness isolates the aspect of the subject, and Reason concerns itself with the unity of subject and object. Within Consciousness, Sense-certainty takes particulars as its objects, Perception deals with universals, and Understanding has as its object 'force', which involves a dynamic inter-relation of particular and universal. All the groups of three can be analysed in this way. And in each case the third stage reconciles the opposites in a way which is itself still one-sided, so that a new triad is generated.

However, as Hegel says of Kant, we have as yet identified only the lifeless external schema. We have now to look at the living movement of thought which lies behind it.

1. Figures presented in this way indicate page numbers and line numbers. All page references, unless otherwise stated, are to G.W.F. Hegel: *The Phenomenology of Mind,* translated by J.B. Baillie, 2nd edition, London 1931. When quoting from the text I shall sometimes alter Baillie's translation considerably.

2. In order to retain the Kantain reference, it is important to translate 'was Ansich ist' as 'what is *in-itself*'. Baillie has 'what exists per se', and elsewhere translates the term 'Ansichseyn' by such phrases as 'inherent and essential reality', 'what is implicitly real' and so on, instead of 'being-in-itself'. Equally misleading is his translation of 'Fursichseyn' (being-for-itself) as 'self-existence', 'what is explicit', or 'being on its own account'. When reading Baillie's translation it is necessary to look out for these phrases.

   Notice also that at the very beginning of the Introduction Hegel's portentous-sounding term 'the Absolute' has been introduced, and seems to mean simply 'reality' or 'things as they are in themselves'.

3. Hegel's use of the term 'science' needs noting. It is wider than the normal English use of the word 'science', which is confined to the natural sciences, and to other areas of knowledge insofar as they are modelled on the natural sciences. Hegel's own conception of science will emerge. For the time being we should simply note that he uses the word to mean 'rigorous and systematic knowledge of reality.'

   Hegel regards his own philosophical system as science. His most general presentation of his philosophy is called the 'Encyclopaedia of the Philosophical Sciences', and its first section is entitled 'The Science of Logic'.

4. L. Wittgenstein: *Philosophical Investigations* paras. 198-242.

5. M. Merleau-Ponty: *The Phenemenology of Perception* p. viii. L. Wittgenstein: *Op.cit.,* paras. 654-5.

6. Hegel does not mention Descartes by name, but this description, and the allusion to the *cogito* in the last clause, make the reference obvious. At the same time we should remember that Cartesian doubt is not confined to Descartes. The same approach is to be found, for example, in the British empiricists.

7. As recommended and defended by Kaufmann, in his *Hegel* p. 369f.

8. Such a procedure does however raise one general problem. If the criticism of each form of consciousness consists in discovering a failure of correspondence between subject and object, why should it have been supposed that such a correspondence existed in the first place? If, for example, 'sense-certainty' turns out not to be an adequate description of our knowledge of immediate sensory particulars, on what basis was it adopted in the first place as a description of the form of knowledge which we set out to examine? Hegel will have to claim that the initial characterisation of each form of knowledge always 'has a certain truth', even though it subsequently proves to be inadequate. What more precise sense we can attach to this claim remains to be seen.

9. Kenley Royce Dove, in an article on 'Hegel's Phenomenological Method' (esp. p.56) reads a great deal more into this sentence — more, I think, than the text will sustain.

10. *Cf. Phenomenology* p. 459.

11. *Cf. Phenomenology* pp. 689-690.

12. J.N. Findlay: *Hegel — A Re-examination* pp. 69f.

2

KNOWLEDGE AND EXPERIENCE

1. Hegel begins where many philosophers have begun, with the idea that the most authentic form of knowledge is direct sensory awareness of particulars. He calls this attitude 'Sense-certainty'.

The section on Sense-certainty has a structure which recurs, though often in a more complicated form, in all the succeeding sections. It begins with an initial presentation of this kind of consciousness. This is written from the standpoint of the philosophical 'we', who already recognise the contradictions inherent in this description. There follows the central dialectical section, in which we 'look on' and observe how these contradictions become apparent in the course of the experience of sense-certainty. Finally there is a concluding section in which 'we' perform the function indicated in the Introduction, that of making explicit the nature of the new object implied by the outcome of the dialectic.

2. Why does Hegel take this kind of knowledge as his starting-point?

'The knowledge which is at the start or immediately our object can be nothing else than just that which is immediate knowledge.' (p. 149)

The idea of sense-certainty as 'direct' or 'immediate' knowledge is a common one; but Hegel needs to give some further account of it, since the contrasted notion of 'mediation' is for him an important one. His further explanation of 'immediate' knowledge is this:

'I, *this* particular conscious I, am certain of *this* fact before me, not because I *qua* consciousness have developed myself in connection with it and in manifold ways set thought to work about it; and not, again, because the fact, the thing, of which I am certain, in virtue of its having a multitude of distinct qualities, was replete with possible modes of relation and a variety of other things.' (pp. 149-150)

There are two ideas here: the one, that such knowledge is entirely

29

passive and that consciousness does not actively work upon its object; the other, that its object is considered entirely in itself, without any relation to other objects. This second point carries the implication that the object is a bare *particular*. As the above description indicates, sense-certainty appears to be a relation between two particulars, regarded purely as particulars – 'I', the subject, and 'this', the object.

In the previous chapter we raised the question whether Hegel's discussions are intended to be primarily of forms of actual experience, or of philosophical theories about experience. We shall have to ask this question about Sense-certainty, but for the moment I shall leave the question open and preserve, in my own account, the ambiguity which is present in Hegel's discussion. We have already indicated, however, that Hegel's description of Sense-certainty is clearly reminiscent of familiar philosophical positions: Greek theories of knowledge such as that discussed by Plato in his *Theaetetus* and that maintained by Epicurus; the philosophy of the British empiricists; or the sensationalism of the French Enlightenment philosophers – a connection which Hegel explicitly makes in the later section on the Enlightenment (p. 577).

Perhaps the most striking resemblance is to more recent version of empiricism – those of Russell and of the logical positivists. In a characteristic essay entitled 'Knowledge by Acquaintance and Knowledge by Description', Russell claims that all knowledge of what is known by description is ultimately reducible to knowledge of what is known by direct acquaintance; that sense-data are the most obvious example of objects which we know by direct acquaintance; that most common words, even proper names, are really descriptions, and that there are only two words which are strictly proper names of particulars, namely, 'I' and 'this'.[1]

There are nevertheless also important differences between Russell's position and Hegel's Sense-certainty. Russell, for example, thinks that we can also have knowledge of universals by direct acquaintance. Moreover, the 'sense-data' with which he thinks we are acquainted are not physical objects, but colours, sounds, etc. The initial objects of Hegel's Sense-certainty are physical objects such as trees and houses; but Hegel subsequently reveals the way in which the description of Sense-certainty requires a retreat into a typical sense-datum theory.

3. The dialectical or critical section of 'Sense-certainty' itself has three sub-sections: one $(151^{23} - 153^{19})$ in which the object of sense-certainty is taken to be the essential element; a second $(153^{20} - 154^{35})$ in which the subject, the knowing self, is taken to be the essential element;

and a third $(154^{36} - 158^2)$ in which the subject-object complex is treated as whole and undivided.

If the object is made the essential element, this kind of experience involves the claim that certainty is possible insofar as the object of sensation is a 'This', a particular. 'This' may refer either to a particular point in time, a 'now', or to a particular location in space, a 'here'.

> 'To the question "What is the Now?" we reply, for example "The Now is night". To test the truth of this certainty of sense, a simple experiment is all we need: write that truth down. A truth cannot lose anything by being written down. . . . If we look again at the truth we have written down, look at it *now, at midday,* we shall have to say that it has turned stale and become out of date. . . . The same will be the case when we take the Here, the other form of the This. The Here is e.g. the tree. I turn round and this truth has disappeared and changed into its opposite: the Here is not a tree, but a house.' (pp. 151–3)

This criticism is deceptively whimsical. It looks as though it is simply a play on the use of tenses. The serious point, however, concerns the use of the terms 'this', 'here' and 'now'. What becomes apparent is that 'now' can refer equally to night or to midday, 'here' can refer equally to a house or a tree. So far from being the names of particulars, they are the most universal terms of all, for they can refer indifferently to absolutely anything while retaining the same meaning throughout. The conclusion to be drawn is not that the wrong terms have been chosen, it is that *no* terms are simply the names of particulars. Language is inherently universal. It is characteristic of *any* word that it is used with the *same* meaning on *different* occasions, and therefore that there must be features common to the different occasions which entitle us to use the same word. Consequently language cannot do what the idea of 'sense-certainty' requires – *simply* pick out particulars.

> '. . . we utter what is universal; in other words, we do not actually say what, in this sense-certainty, we really *mean*. . . . It is not possible for us even to express any sensuous existence which we 'mean'. (p. 152)

That is Hegel's argument. We might envisage the reply 'Why does sense-certainty need to be expressed in language at all? Perhaps it is characteristic of just this kind of consciousness that its content cannot be formulated in words.'[2] There are two points which can be made here. The first is that, if the content of sense-certainty cannot be expressed in language, it cannot properly be described as *knowledge*. It is of the essence of knowledge that it is capable of being shared and communicated, of being presented for agreement or refutation. Only on this condition can it be seen as 'rational'; only on this condition can the notions of truth and falsity be applicable to it. Hints of such an argument can be found at the end of the Sense-certainty section, where Hegel says:

'What is called "unspeakable" is nothing else than what is untrue, irrational. . .' (p. 160)

Also relevant is a passage in the Preface:

'[When] the man of common sense appeals to his feeling, to an oracle within his breast, he is done with any one who does not agree. He has to explain that he has no more to say to any one who does not find and feel the same as himself. In other words, he tramples the roots of humanity underfoot. For the nature of humanity is to impel men to agree with one another, and its very existence lies simply in the implicit realization of a community of conscious life.' (p. 127)

The second and more far-reaching point which can be made is that the particulars which are the supposed objects of sense-certainty cannot even be identified as particulars without the use of language and universal terms. Suppose that I point to 'this' which is in front of me. Do I mean this room? this wall? this area of wall? this patch of light? this colour? The 'particular' to which the 'this' refers can be picked out only insofar as it is brought under some universal term. A 'particular' is necessarily a particular something, a particular of a certain kind. This argument too is employed by Hegel in what follows.

4. I say 'in what follows'. We might have expected the treatment of Sense-certainty to end at this point. The inadequacy of the initial characterisation has been indicated and, as we might gather from the Introduction, there can now be a transition to a new form of consciousness. But such a transition does not yet occur. Instead, attempts are made to shore up the present form of consciousness, and these are in their turn subjected to criticism.

The first suggestion is that the notion of sense-certainty can be preserved if we suppose the guarantee of certainty to be located not in the object of experience but in the subject:

'Its truth lies in the object as *my* object, . . . in what I *mean*; it *is*, because *I* know it. Sense-certainty is thus indeed banished from the object, but it is not yet thereby done away with; it is merely forced back into the I.' (p. 153)

This move parallels the way in which twentieth-century philosophers have often tried to preserve the essentials of a sense-datum theory. For example G. J. Warnock, in his book on Berkeley, suggests that we can make sense of Berkeley's theory of perception not by supposing that there is some special class of entities ('ideas') which are the objects of 'immediate perception', but rather by understanding statements of immediate perception as statements which are incorrigible simply because they involve no claim which is open to refutation by future investigations. The statement 'I hear a car' cannot count as a statement of immediate perception, since it could readily turn out to be false. But a statement such as 'I hear a sort of purring noise' is no better in this respect; we do not achieve incorrigibility by talking about sounds (colours, tastes etc.) instead of physical objects, for statements about the former may equally turn out to be false. Even the statement 'I hear what sounds to me like a purring noise' is not incorrigible, since I may actually be hearing nothing at all. But if I simply say 'It seems to me now as if I were hearing a sort of purring noise', this, according to Warnock, *is* incorrigible and can therefore count as a statement of immediate perception. It is, he says, incorrigible because I am not making any claim about what *is actually the case*, I am simply stating how things *seem to me*.[3] The revised attitude of sense-certainty, analogously, can be presented as the assertion that the richest, truest and most authentic knowledge-claims are those whose certainty is guaranteed by their referring solely to 'how things seem to me'.

Hegel's criticism of this revised position is rather obscure. It appears to turn on the fact that such a position involves an untenable solipsism. Hegel says:

'I, *this* I, see the tree, and assert the tree to be the Here; *another* I, however, sees the house and maintains the Here is not a tree but a house. Both truths have the same authenticity, which consists in the immediacy of the seeing, and in the certainty and assurance which each possesses concerning its knowledge; but the one certainty disappears in the other. In all this, what does not disappear is the I *qua* universal whose seeing is neither the seeing of this tree nor of this house, but simply seeing as such. . . . I is merely universal, like Now, Here, or This in general.' (p. 154)

I would interpret this along the following lines. The revised attitude of sense-certainty requires me to treat all knowledge-claims as reducible to claims about what seems to me to be the case. They must all be re-interpreted in terms of a reference to my own immediate experience. But this amounts to a solipsistic view of knowledge – 'The world is my world' – and therefore involves treating 'I' purely and simply as the name of a unique particular. In fact however the term 'I' cannot, any more than the term 'this', be treated as a pure particular. Insofar as it can be used by any language user, it can refer indifferently to *any* self. The 'I' is identifiable only as one among many 'I's. Therefore the use of the term 'I', and of language generally, commits one to the recognition that the same language can be used by other language users, and thus that claims about what *I* know or what *I* experience are potentially open to being shared in by others or being opposed by their competing claims. The use of 'I' commits one to the existence of other selves, other subjects of sense-experience, and their experience may or may not agree with one's own.

This is a considerable expansion of Hegel's argument. It may be that I have read into it more than I should. But I should like to think that this is what Hegel means, because I consider that such an argument would be correct.

5. The third and final dialectical section deals with the attempt to retain the attitude of sense-certainty by means of one further retreat. Certainty is now taken to reside neither in a certain kind of object nor in the reference to a self, but rather in a simple experience confined to a single particular point in space and time. Any reference to a continuing object or to a continuing self is jettisoned, and the suggestion is that so long as the experience is regarded simply by itself, without reference to anything else, certainty is guaranteed.

'Sense-certainty discovers by experience. . .that its essential nature lies neither in the object nor in the I. . . . Its truth stands fast as a self-identical relation making no distinction of essential and non-essential, between I and object. . . .I, *this* I, assert, then, the Here as tree, . . .and take no notice of the fact that another I finds the Here as not-tree, or that I myself at some other time take the Here as not-tree, the Now as not-day. . . .I take my stand on *one* immediate relation: the Now is day.' (pp. 154-5)

Once again, a contemporary comparison is available. A.J. Ayer, in *Language, Truth and Logic,* suggests that the notion of a 'sense-content' should not be analysed in terms of a subject and an object but should be taken to refer to the occurrence of a simple experience. And of such experiences he says:

> 'There is a class of empirical propositions of which it is permissible to say that they can be verified conclusively. . . .They refer solely to the content of a single experience. . . .In a verbal sense, indeed, it is always possible to misdescribe one's experience; but if one intends to do no more than record what is experienced without relating it to anything else, then it is not possible to be factually mistaken; and the reason for this is that one is making no claim that any further fact could confute.' (*Language, Truth and Logic,* second edition, p. 10)

The crucial suggestion here, as in the attitude which Hegel is considering, is that 'one intends to do no more than record what is experienced without relating it to anything else.' It is this that Hegel regards as impossible.

The argument initially seems to turn on the impossibility of absolute instants of space and time. If 'Here' or 'Now' is to refer to a pure particular unrelated to any other, it can be identified only by being pointed out. But in the time that it takes to utter the word 'Now', the point in time which it is supposed to pick out has already passed. That point in time can of course still be identified, but not as something 'immediate'. It can be identified only in relation to other points in time, as one 'Now' among others. The force of this argument is clarified by the analogous argument about 'Here':

> 'The Here pointed out, which I keep hold of, is likewise a *this* Here which, in fact, is not *this Here,* but a Before and Behind, an Above and Below, a Right and Left.' (p. 157)

We can therefore suppose Hegel to have been arguing, similarly, that the 'Now' can be identified not by some kind of inner ostension but only as 'before such-and-such', 'after such-and-such' — in other words, by reference to events and thus to other points in time. Consequently, one cannot in fact record an 'immediate' experience 'without relating it to anything else'. And we can see that this applies not just to particular points in space and time but to any supposed 'immediate particulars'. In recording an experience as being, for example, an experience of a certain colour I am, just by applying a descriptive term to it, identifying it as like certain other colour-experiences, and also unlike others. The argument is in effect the one which I mentioned above (p. 32) and which I said we would find Hegel employing: particulars cannot even be identified without the use of universal terms.

6. Since this brings us to the end of the dialectical or critical section, it is time to confront explicitly the question which we have so far evaded: what exactly is it that Hegel is criticising here? Is it the actual experience of sense-certainty, or a philosophical theory about it?

There can be no doubt that Hegel's discussion is *at least* intended as a criticism of certain philosophical doctrines. He says this in so many words (p.158[11-20]). However, the view of experience which has been criticised has, throughout, been attributed by Hegel not simply to the philosophers but to 'consciousness'. In keeping with his idea that consciousness does all the work whilst we simply look on, Hegel constantly talks of 'sense-certainty' or 'consciousness' or 'the naive consciousness' declaring itself to be such-and-such, finding by experience that it is mistaken about itself, and so on.

In what sense, then, is the naive consciousness mistaken? Does Hegel mean that whenever, in our everyday experience, we lay claim to certainty about what we can see and hear, our claims are illegitimate? Not exactly. For in one sense it is perfectly true and undeniable that we can often be 'certain' about 'particular' things which we can see 'directly'. I know that I am at present sitting in front of a desk, and how could I doubt it when I can see it 'with my own eyes'. But what Hegel has shown is that such an experience cannot be described as *simply* a 'direct' awareness of 'particulars'. It is 'direct' knowledge in contrast to what I know at second-hand – to what I know because I have read it or because others have told me. But it is not 'direct' or 'immediate' knowledge in an absolute sense. It is not, as Russell would have it, simply the 'presentation' of an object. The 'immediate' object of knowledge is at the same time 'mediated' – by language, and by its relations to other objects. Similarly Hegel has shown that particulars are not just bare particulars; they are at the same time universals, and cannot in fact be the one without the other. When the naive consciousness, then, claims to be 'certain' about 'this' which it can see 'directly', its description of its experience is, from a philosophical point of view, inadequate because incomplete. It is false when taken in isolation, cut off from its opposite.

7. The most important element in Hegel's criticism of Sense-certainty is,

I think, the assertion of the importance of language. The 'immediate' objects of sense-certainty are identified by means of language; and it is this fact which contradicts the account of immediacy given at the beginning of the section (p. 149; see above, p. 29f.). Consciousness *does* 'develop itself in connection with its object', it *does* 'set thought to work about it'. Consciousness is active even within the experience of sense-certainty, for it does not passively receive the objects which are presented to it, but characterises them, brings them under universal concepts. In Russellian terms, there is no knowledge by acquaintance which is not also knowledge by description.

An interesting elaboration of this point comes in the later section on 'Observation of Nature' (the initial stages of which cover the same ground as the stages of 'Consciousness'). The passage begins thus:

> 'When the unreflective consciousness speaks of observation and experience as being the fountain of truth, the phrase may possibly sound as if the whole business were a matter of tasting, smelling, feeling, hearing, and seeing. It forgets, in its zeal for tasting, smelling, etc., to say that, in point of fact, it has really and rationally determined for itself already the object thus sensuously apprehended, and this determination of the object is at least as important for it as that apprehension.' (p. 284)

It is this emphasis on the necessity of bringing the sensuous manifold under 'determinations', ordering it by means of concepts, that leads to Hegel's further claim that the objects of sensuous apprehension are not just particulars but at the same time also universals. At the end of the section on 'Sense-certainty', this becomes the point of transition to a new form of consciousness. The objects of consciousness are universals. Consequently our awareness of them is not just an immediate apprehension. It is a new form of consciousness, which will be called 'Perception' — an awareness of objects as things possessing properties, where these properties are universals common to many particulars.

The section thus ends, as we were given to expect, with the philosophical narrator making explicit the new form of consciousness which is implicit in the critique of the old form. But the pattern of the dialectical critique has in fact been more complex than we were led to suppose. The pattern which seemed to be suggested in Hegel's Introduction could be represented as follows:

$$S_1 \qquad O_1$$

$$S_2 \qquad O_2$$

That is to say: we are initially presented with a certain form of consciousness consisting in a relation between a certain kind of object (O_1) and a certain kind of subject (S_1). But given the description of the object as O_1, the description of the subject as S_1 turns out to be inadequate, and the subject has to be re-described as S_2. This re-description of the subject, however, carries with it a new conception of the object, as O_2; and the relation between S_2 and O_2 constitutes a new form of consciousness (Cf. *Phenomenology* pp. 140-2, and Ch. 1 above, p. 20).

However, the pattern in sense-certainty has been the more elaborate one which can be represented thus:

$$S_1 \qquad O_1$$

$$S_2 \qquad O_2$$

$$S_3 \qquad O_3$$

$$S_4 \qquad O_4$$

That is to say: The certainty of sensuous knowledge is at first supposed to be guaranteed by the nature of the object as a pure particular, a 'Here' or a 'Now' (O_1). The object is therefore the essential element in the relation, and the subject (S_1) is the non-essential. However, the object, the 'Now' or the 'Here', cannot in fact be a bare particular; it is at the same time a universal (O_2). Therefore the certainty in our sensuous knowledge of it can be guaranteed only by the referring of all such knowledge to a unique particular subject of experience, the 'I' (S_2). However, the 'I' also turns out to be not just a bare particular but a universal (S_3). It is therefore capable of certainty only if it is confined to a single isolated experience whose object is a unique instant, a single isolated point in space and time (O_3). However, such a unique instant is an impossibility; it is in reality a 'now' in relation to other nows, a 'here' in relation to other heres — a universal (O_4). The experience of such a universal is 'perception' (S_4).

8. I shall discuss only briefly the sections on 'Perception' and 'Force and Understanding', in which Hegel continues to deal, though less rewardingly, with traditional epistemological problems. 'Sense-certainty' ended by demonstrating the necessity of the category of 'universals', and 'Perception' takes up this problem, identifying 'universals' with the *properties* which things have in common. Hegel's discussion revolves around the relation between 'things' and their 'properties', and can usefully be seen as developing some of the dilemmas and ambiguities in Locke's account of substance.[4] Locke frequently proclaims, on epistemological grounds, that a 'thing' cannot be anything other than a collection of qualities, but he also recognises that this is not what is normally meant by a 'thing'; a 'thing' must have a *unity* and be more than just a collection. Upon this ambivalence, Hegel's treatment of Perception is built. The thing must be no more than the sum of its properties, a mere 'also', as Hegel puts it — a block of salt is white and *also* cubical and *also* sharp-tasting, and so on. But these properties can be recognised for what they are only insofar as they can be *contrasted* with *other* properties, and for this to be possible, they have to be identified as the properties of *this thing* in contrast to other things. In the course of the section Hegel takes himself to have shown that neither the category of 'things' nor that of 'properties' can be taken as basic; they are both equally essential, and necessarily involve one another. Similarly, a thing is equally a 'unity' and a 'plurality'. And what a thing is 'for itself' is inseparable from what it is 'for another', i.e. in relation to other things and their properties.

Consciousness now adopts a new conception of its object in which this dynamic inter-relation of opposites is given greater recognition. Such a concept is that of 'force'. A force is in itself something unitary, but it expresses itself in a multiplicity of different ways. The force *becomes* its various expressions, the one *becomes* many. And the form of consciousness which has 'force' as its object is what Hegel calls 'Understanding'.

In his discussion of 'Force and Understanding' Hegel seems mainly to have in mind the concepts and methods of Newtonian physics, and the philosophical treatment of them in the empiricist tradition. In the manner of the previous sections, he points to the necessary inter-relations of such pairs of concepts as 'force' and its 'expression', 'inciting force' and 'incited force', 'force' and 'law', 'reality' and 'appearance'. This last pair is perhaps the most interesting and will serve as an example of Hegel's whole approach. Having shown that 'force' and its 'expression', 'inciting force' and 'incited force', are all equally essential as different manifestations of force, Hegel envisages the suggestion that the true nature of force must be some inner reality behind all these appearances. He continues:

'A supersensible world. . .henceforth opens up as the true world, lying beyond the sensuous world which is the world of appearance. Away remote from the changing vanishing present lies the permanent beyond: an 'in-itself' which is. . .the pure element where the truth finds its abode and its essential being.' (p. 191)

The notion of an 'in-itself' behind appearances has obvious Kantian connotations. At the same time it is wider than that. It represents a philosophical tradition which goes back at least to Parmenides. It is familiar also as a religious idea, and Hegel's vocabulary is deliberately chosen with all these allusions in mind.

In the next paragraph, however, Hegel hints more strongly at a link with Kant. This 'inner reality' has so far, he says, been defined simply as 'not appearance' – a bare 'in-itself' having no positive content. And 'this type of inwardness suits those who say that the inner being of things cannot be known' (p. 192). This is of course precisely what Kant does say about 'things in themselves', and in the Introduction we saw that Hegel was very much concerned to overcome this kind of Kantian scepticism. Consequently it is not surprising that, on the present occasion, the Kantian interpretation of the appearance/reality dichotomy is roundly rejected.

We need, says Hegel, to remind ourselves how this dichotomy has arisen. We were originally led to postulate an inner reality not just as something *other than* appearance, but also as the *truth* of appearance. And so, conversely, appearance is not *mere* appearance; it is never simply illusion. It is always an appearance *of* something, and the nature of that 'something' is therefore to be arrived at by way of its appearances. The appearances *mediate* between us and the inner reality. In short, the concepts of 'appearance' and 'inner reality' are distorted if they are employed in Kantian fashion to denote an absolute dichotomy. Inner reality is the truth of appearance, and appearance is the appearance of inner reality. Accordingly, in the present case, the 'inner reality' behind the play of forces is the truth to which we are pointed by that appearance. The truth of the interaction of forces is a realm of scientific *laws*.

Hegel's discussion of 'appearance' and 'reality' is thus a further instance of his claim that opposed concepts are not simply abstract and separated opposites, but that each is intelligible only in the light of the other. Throughout the three sections of 'Consciousness' Hegel's theme has been the recognition that opposites coalesce – particular and universal, unity and plurality, force and expression, appearance and reality, etc. Towards the end of 'Understanding' he formulates this in the statement: 'We have to think pure flux, *opposition within itself,* or *contradiction'* (p.206). Particulars are at the same time universals – it is in this sense that Hegel thinks it necessary to recognise the existence of contradiction. Since, however, many philosophers have found unpalatable the suggestion that reality contains contradictions, it may be worth considering other ways in which Hegel formulates this same conclusion.

9. At the end of the 'Perception' section Hegel says:

'These empty abstractions of 'singleness' and its antithetic 'universality', of 'essential' . . . and 'non-essential' . . . are powers the interplay of which constitutes perceptual understanding, often called 'sound common sense' (Menschenverstand). This 'healthy common sense', which takes itself to be the solid substantial type of conscious life, is, in its process of perception, merely the sport of these abstractions. . . . It is tossed about by these unreal entities, bandied from one to the other, and by its sophistry endeavours to affirm and hold fast alternatively now one, then the exact opposite. . . . In each particular moment it is merely conscious of one given characteristic as the truth, and then, again, of the opposite.' (pp. 176-8)

The fact that Hegel talks indiscriminately of both 'perception' and 'understanding', and that he also refers elsewhere in the same paragraph to 'sense-certainty', indicates that he is here offering a general characterisation of all these first three stages of the *Phenemenology*. As Baillie's translation reveals, the term 'Menschenverstand' links these with the attitudes of everyday 'common-sense'; and the same term reminds us that Locke's 'human understanding' is seen by Hegel as the philosophical equivalent of this form of consciousness. Hegel regularly uses the term 'understanding' (which, following Kant, he contrasts with 'reason') in this wider sense to denote common sense and its formalisation in empiricist philosophy.

What Hegel takes to be characteristic of the understanding is that, when confronted with the traditional philosophical opposites (and to those already mentioned we could add many others, e.g. form and content, mind and matter, individual and society, freedom and necessity) it operates on a principle of 'either/or'. *Either* one term of the opposed pair is more fundamental *or* the other is. Thus the understanding is typically *reductionist*: the only reality is that of particulars, and universals are simply fashioned by the mind from its experience of particulars; physical objects are simply collections of observable properties (or logical constructions out of sense-data, or whatever); statements about forces are reducible to statements about their observable expression (cf. the Humean view of causality); a society is simply a collection of individuals, and so on. Hegel rejects such reductionism. In every case he claims to show that A cannot be reducible to B, since B itself presupposes A and is unintelligible without it. Universals cannot be reducible to particulars, since particulars are themselves identifiable only insofar as they are also universals. Physical objects cannot be reducible to observable properties, since such properties are identifiable only as the properties of individual objects; and so on.

At the same time Hegel also rejects a reductionism operating in the other direction, that of dogmatic metaphysics. As we have seen, he denies that the world of appearances is ever *mere* appearance. When Parmenides claims that the world of change and plurality is sheer illusion, in contrast to the one changeless reality, or when Schopenhauer similarly contrasts specific causal relationships between individual objects in space and time with the single eternal and undifferentiated 'will' which is the true reality, they are being as one-sided as the reductionist empiricists. 'Reality' cannot be cut off from the forms in which it 'appears'.

Nor, finally, is Hegel a dualist. He does not simply assert that, for example, there are *both* particulars *and* universals, in the manner of, say, Plato or Russell. It is for him essential to understand the opposites not as separate entities but in their interconnection.

Hegel is concerned to emphasise not only the relation between a concept and its opposite, but also the *systematic* interrelation of concepts. The course of the experience of Consciousness has revealed not only the interconnections between 'particular' and 'universal', between 'thing' and 'property', but also the connections between each pair of concepts and the next. It has revealed, in fact, a systematic *structure* of concepts, each of which can be understood not in isolation but only in terms of its relations to the other concepts. The results of this experience could be set out in Kantian fashion as a system of connected categories – and this is how Hegel presents them in his *Logic*.

We can now return to the conclusion of the 'Understanding' section and attempt a further explanation of what Hegel says there. Having introduced the notion of 'internal opposition' or 'contradiction' (A is at the same time the opposite of A) he adds that this relationship between opposed terms can be described as an 'infinity'. This puzzling term can, I think, be explained by reference to the previous notion of an interconnected system of concepts. The term 'infinite' normally suggests an endless progression – the endless succession of the natural numbers, for example, or the indefinite extendability of a straight line. But this is not what Hegel means here by 'infinity'; he calls it elsewhere (in the *Logic*) a 'bad' or 'false' infinity. What then is a 'true' infinity? We can perhaps explain it by saying that it consists not in the absence of external limits but in the absence of *internal* limits. A finite entity becomes an element in an infinity, in this sense, not by being endlessly repeated but by being understood in its relations to all the other entities with which it is connected. The absence of internal limits means that this finite entity is not taken in isolation, cut off from its relations with everything. So, again, the emphasis is on the existence of an interconnected system.

In using the term 'infinity' to convey this idea, Hegel no doubt has in mind the traditional aspiration of religion and of philosophy to go beyond a knowledge of the finite to a knowledge of the infinite. If this infinite is literally a 'beyond', another world set over against the finite, then it is just as limited and one-sided as the finite. The important way in which our knowledge *can* go beyond the finite is by abandoning the attitude which says that 'everything is what it is and not another thing', and by understanding its objects as elements in a whole. As Hegel puts it graphically in the *Logic*, whereas the image of the false infinity is a straight line indefinitely extended, the image of the true infinity is a circle.

Other Hegelian terms can usefully be introduced at this point. Hegel's use of the term 'abstraction', for example, is part of the same emphasis. For Hegel, an idea is 'abstract' not in being over-generalised, but in being cut off – abstracted – from its relations to the other concepts which make it intelligible. Sense-certainty, concerning itself as it does with particulars, is the most abstract form of cognition, since it purports to take its object in complete isolation. Introducing another pair of Hegelian terms, we can say that concepts require to be understood not in abstraction but as 'moments' in a 'totality'. Consider the following comment on Locke from Hegel's *Lectures on the History of Philosophy*:

'When "experience" means that the Concept has objective reality for consciousness, it is indeed a necessary element in the totality; but as this reflection appears in Locke, signifying as it does that we obtain truth by abstraction from experience and sense-perception, it is utterly false since, instead of being a moment, it is made the essence of the truth.' (Op. cit., Vol.III, p. 295)

It is characteristic of empiricism to distinguish between knowledge derived from experience and *a priori* (speculative, conceptual) knowledge, and to champion the former as against the latter. But 'experience' is itself impossible without concepts, and the very attempt to gain knowledge from experience involves us in considering what are the appropriate concepts with which to characterise that experience. There is no absolute dichotomy between 'empirical enquiry' and 'conceptual enquiry'. The 'empirical' and the 'conceptual' are equally essential moments in the totality; each requires the other to complete it.

Finally, the term 'dialectic' (which I have already been using without much explanation and which will have to be discussed at greater length in a later chapter) can be seen as the dynamic aspect of 'totality'. Given the systematic interrelation of concepts within the totality, the attempt to understand a concept will lead to a recognition of how it is inseparable, first, from its opposite, and then from all the other concepts. This has been the course taken by experience throughout this first part of the *Phenomenology*. More dramatically, Hegel describes such experience as 'pure flux', 'absolute unrest'. And the term 'dialectical' can, for the time being, be understood as a way of referring to this aspect of experience.

10. The section on Consciousness ends with a transition to Self-consciousness, and thus the upshot of the whole section is that, in some sense or other, 'consciousness of an other, of an object in general, is indeed itself necessarily self-consciousness' (p. 211). In *what* sense, exactly? At certain points Hegel has emphasised the *active* nature of consciousness. In Sense-certainty he showed that consciousness must apply *language* to its object, and that to this extent sense-certainty cannot be purely immediate knowledge; consciousness must *work* on its object (see above, p. 37). Similarly in the discussion of the 'inner world' it was shown that this inner world is not an empty beyond, but is the truth of appearance; consciousness has to postulate an inner reality behind appearances in order to make sense of the appearances,

and in this sense consciousness itself provides the inner world with its content.

> 'It is manifest that behind the so-called curtain which is to hide the inner world, there is nothing to be seen unless we ourselves go behind there, both in order that we may thereby see, and that there may be something behind there which can be seen.' (p. 212)

This stress on the *activity* of consciousness is in fact implicit in the whole emphasis on *concepts* — those concepts such as 'universal' and 'particular', 'thing' and 'property', 'force', etc. whose discovery has been the overriding theme. These concepts are the production of consciousness, and therefore in knowing them consciousness knows itself.[5]

---

[1] B. Russell: *Logic and Mysticism* esp. pp. 158, 153, 156 and 162.

[2] This objection seems to have been first formulated by Feuerbach in his *Critique of Hegel's Philosophy* (see *The Fiery Brook: Selected Writings of Ludwig Feuerbach*, pp. 76-9). The same objection can also be found in J. Maier: *On Hegel's Critique of Kant*, pp. 76ff., and J. Loewenberg: 'The Commedy of Immediacy in Hegel's "Phenomenology"', pp. 25 and 36.

[3] G. J. Warnock: *Berkeley* pp. 158-163.

[4] See Locke: *Essay Concerning Human Understanding*, Bk. II, ch. XXIII.

[5] *Cf. Phenomenology* pp. 565f.: 'The absolute concept is the category; it is the principle that knowledge and the object of knowledge are the same. . . . What is not rational has no truth; what is not conceptually comprehended, *is* not. When reason thus speaks of some *other* than itself, it in fact speaks merely of itself; it does not therein go beyond itself.'

3

SELF-REALISATION AND
THE MASTER-SLAVE RELATION

1. The structure of 'Self-consciousness' is parallel to that of 'Consciousness' — a parallel which Hegel needlessly obscures by his erratic system of numbering. Corresponding to the three sections of 'Consciousness', the sections of 'Self-consciousness' are:

IV.   The Truth of Self-certainty;

IV.A.   Dependence and Independence of Self-Consciousness: Master and Slave;

IV.B.   Freedom of Self-consciousness: Stoicism, Scepticism and the Unhappy Consciousness.

The section on 'Self-certainty' is extremely unrewarding, and since I find large parts of it unintelligible I shall say little about it. The one important point to be gleaned from it is the claim that in order to be conscious of one's own existence one must experience *desire*. Desire is the most basic and immediate form of self-consciousness, which Hegel therefore refers to as 'self-certainty'. He fails to make it clear why desire should have this importance, but an argument can easily be supplied. So long as my consciousness is purely contemplative, no distinction can arise for me between the objects which make up the content of my awareness and 'I' who am aware of them. But once there is a contrast between the world of which I am aware and the world as I want it to be, and once I act on the world in order to make it conform to my desires, I may acquire some minimal consciousness of myself as something distinct from the rest of my world. In other words I must be aware of a conflict between myself and my world in order to be able to distinguish the two.

The experience of desire, however, does not constitute self-consciousness in the full sense. Why is this? In 'Self-certainty' Hegel offers a preliminary explanation, but the whole question is dealt with much more satisfactorily in the 'Master and Slave' section, to which we may now gratefully turn.

2.   'Self-consciousness is initially simple being-for-itself, self-identity by

exclusion of every other from itself. . . . But the other is also a self-consciousness; an individual makes its appearance in antithesis to an individual. Appearing thus in their immediacy, they are for each other in the manner of ordinary objects. . . . Each is indeed certain of its own self, but not of the other, and hence its own certainty of itself is still without truth. . . . They must bring their certainty of themselves, the certainty of being for themselves, to the level of objective truth.' (pp. 231-2).

Hegel's claim here is that one cannot be fully conscious of oneself, as a self, unless one is aware of others as selves. The rudimentary form of self-consciousness which he has called 'self-certainty', and which he has linked with the experience of desire, is inadequate because at this level one's awareness of oneself would lack objectivity. What is necessary is that one should, in some sense, be aware of oneself as one self among other selves. Self-certainty, in contrast, is a purely solipsistic self-consciousness.

In order to see the force of Hegel's claim, let us imagine a human being who has always lived in complete isolation and is unaware of the existence of other human beings. The hypothesis is a frequent object of philosophical speculation. Begging certain questions about it, let us suppose that this being is able to act on the world in various ways, to gather plants and perhaps kill other animals for food, to use foliage and timber and stones to provide himself with shelter, and so on. Such a being might be regarded as conscious of himself in the minimal sense that he is aware of the world as existing for him and in opposition to him, as resisting him and requiring him to act on it. But he could not be aware of himself as an object in the world, in the way in which the plants and animals he feeds on, and the materials he uses, are objects in the world. He could not be aware of himself in this way because he could not be aware of himself as an object of possible awareness for other human beings. This, I think, is Hegel's claim.

If correct, it is not only an important claim about the nature of self-knowledge, but can also be seen as a resolution of the problem of solipsism.[1] To adhere to solipsism would be to assert 'I know of my own existence but not of the existence of others.' But according to Hegel a knowledge of others is necessarily presupposed in anything more than a minimal self-knowledge.

This 'knowledge of self through knowledge of others' has, for Hegel, two aspects. In the first place, I must be aware of others as persons, and thereby recognise in an objective way what it is to be a person. And in order to see *myself* as being equally a person in just this same manner, I must not only recognise others as persons but also be *recognised by them* as a person. Thereby my own existence is given an objective validity.

> 'Self-consciousness exists in and for itself, in that, and by the fact that it exists for another self-consciousness; that is to say, it *is* only by being recognized.' (p. 229).

What does Hegel mean by 'recognition'? When he talks of one self-consciousness 'recognizing' another he must mean more than simply that the one is aware of the other's existence. The details of his account (which we shall look at shortly) indicate that, prior to the attainment of recognition (and particularly in what Hegel will call 'the life-and-death struggle'), he must envisage two self-consciousnesses being 'aware of one another's existence' in this minimal sense. 'Recognition' in the full sense, on the other hand, means being recognised *as a person*; and for Hegel, this means being recognised as an *independent and autonomous agent*.

Hegel's idea of the 'need for recognition' has been developed by existential psychiatrists such as R. D. Laing in ways which help to throw light on Hegel's original concept.[2] Studies by Laing and others exhibit in concrete ways how a person may be denied recognition by others. Actions and utterances which express his own individuality may be persistently ignored or dismissed or systematically re-interpreted. Others may ascribe to him experiences, perceptions and intentions which systematically conflict with and invalidate his own self-attributions. Within a closed institution such as the family this persistent denial of recognition may, quite literally, lead to the disintegration of a person's sense of identity and to a condition of schizophrenia.

Talk of having, or losing, a sense of one's own identity suggests a connection with the traditional philosophical 'problem of personal identity'. Such a connection has often been denied by analytical philosophers. The problem of personal identity, they have said, is simply the question of what entitles us to apply identity-statements to persons. The question is: What are the criteria on the basis of which it can be said that 'the person who did X' and 'the person who did Y' are the same person? (Continuity of consciousness? Bodily continuity?) And this question, it is said, has nothing to do with psychological problems about 'having a sense of identity'.

This, I think, is a mistake. There is no sharp distinction between the two problems. Consider a case of the sort which Laing presents, where a person experiences his thoughts and actions as coming to him from outside, as having a power of their own which is beyond his control. In a sense, he is aware of them all as being *his* thoughts and actions. His doubts are not of a sort which would arise about thoughts and actions belonging quite straightforwardly to other people. And yet, at another level, his doubt *is* a doubt about whether these experiences are really his. His problem has precisely the structure of the 'philosophical' problem of identity: are these various experiences all experiences belonging to a single person? We can, and must, talk of different *levels* at which the problem of identity arises, because there are different levels at which one can be, more or less fully, a person. And it is essential to recognize the continuity between these different levels. There is no simple set of criteria for 'being a person'. At a minimal level, one may be a self-conscious person simply in the sense of being the subject of experiences. As we have seen, a higher level of self-consciousness is reached when, through desire and action, one is able to distinguish between oneself, as the subject of the experiences, and the world of which they are experiences. The subsequent levels of self-consciousness which we are now considering involve a degree of coherence in those experiences which is necessary to being properly a person, and this requires that the coherence be given objective validity through recognition by others. If we are to understand Hegel's discussion of self-consciousness, it is essential to read it not as a sequence of attempts to define self-consciousness, each of which proves abortive and is replaced by another, but rather as a sequence of stages by which one becomes more fully a person, and more fully conscious of oneself as a person.

3. I have been assuming that Hegel's account is to be taken as a general account of the necessary features of any person's consciousness of his own identity. This way of reading it, however, soon runs up against difficulties, which will be apparent from a brief summary of the remainder of the 'Master and Slave' section:

    i. Each self-consciousness aims to be recognised by, and to find itself in, the other. However, insofar as its identity resides in an other, it is outside its own control; it must therefore also aim to destroy the other. And the conflict between them must be a struggle for life and death, since it is only by risking one's life that one is aware of oneself as a free, autonomous individual. (pp. 231^{24}-233^{21})

ii. However, the death of one of the combatants will make it impossible for either of them to be recognised. Recognition is possible only if one of them submits to the other. This creates the relation of master and slave. (pp. 233^{22}-234^{31})

iii. It might seem that the master has now obtained recognition as an independent being. But since this recognition is accorded him by the slave, who is *not* an independent being but merely does his master's will, it does *not* constitute an objective confirmation of the master's identity. (pp. 234^{32}-237^{5})

iv. The slave, on the other hand, realizes himself and objectifies himself through *work* for the master. In shaping and forming the natural world, he can find in the product of his work an objective and lasting expression of his own identity, whereas the master, whose relationship to the natural world is entirely one of desire and consumption, is incapable of doing this. Moreover, the slave has experienced *fear*, fear for his life, and therefore knows that his whole existence has been at stake; through the experience of *service,* this fear has spread itself over his whole life; and consequently he has experienced to the full that consciousness of his own existence which can be given objective expression in *work*. (pp. 237^{6}-240^{19})

The difficulties which this poses are obvious. How can we take it seriously as an account of the necessary conditions of self-consciousness? Who could possibly maintain that one cannot have a proper awareness of one's own identity unless one has risked one's life in war, worked as a slave, and so on? How can these very specific experiences have that general significance which, on our previous reading of Hegel, we seem committed to assigning them?

Some help can be obtained from Hegel's lecture-notes on 'Master and Slave'. (These notes, compiled from Hegel's own and from those of students who attended his lectures, actually refer to the equivalent section in the Encyclopaedia *Philosophy of Mind.*[3]) They suggest that we ought to revise our interpretation, and see Hegel's account of the fight for recognition and the master-slave relation as specifying not the permanently necessary preconditions of self-consciousness, but the form taken by self-consciousness within certain historical periods. Hegel asserts, for example, that the fight for recognition, in its extreme form,

' . . .can only occur in the natural state, where men exist only as single, separate individuals; but it is absent in civil society and the State because here the recognition for which the combatants fought already exists.' (*Philosophy of Mind*, Note to para. 432)

Similarly the relationship of master and slave is seen as a first step from the state of nature to social life, typifying the societies of the ancient world but subsequently giving way to a form of society in which all men are recognised as free (Para. 433 and note).

The re-interpretation of Hegel's account along historical lines certainly makes it more plausible, but it still leaves us with a problem. For, if the experiences which Hegel describes — the life-and-death struggle for recognition, the experience of working in fear and obedience to a master — are no longer necessary in a free society, then what becomes of Hegel's own arguments in the *Phenomenology* purporting to show that such experiences *are* necessary conditions of self-consciousness? He certainly appears to be arguing not just that these experiences had to be gone through in the course of human history, but that, quite literally, one cannot be fully conscious of oneself unless one has risked one's life in battle, feared for one's whole existence, and worked in a condition of service. How then can these arguments be compatible with the assertion that such experiences can be historically superseded?

This last point is taken up by Sartre in a discussion of Hegel and of the 'Master and Slave' section. He accuses Hegel of optimism precisely in supposing that the master-slave relation can be surpassed and that recognition can be mutual. To be known by the Other, he argues, is to be an *object* for the Other, and this is epitomised in the experience of being the object of the Other's *look*. In this situation I cease to experience myself as a free subject apprehending the world in terms of my projects and intentions. I become, in the eyes of the Other, a calculable element in the world, the object of his predictions and assessments. 'It is', says Sartre, 'in this sense that we can consider ourselves as "slaves" in so far as we appear to the Other' (*Being and Nothingness* p. 267). But, he adds, slavery in this sense 'is not a historical result, capable of being surmounted.' It is 'the permanent structure of my being-for-others'. I cannot be known as a subject by the Other, nor can I know myself as an object except insofar as I have the experience of being an object for an Other. Consequently there are only two possible relations between myself and the Other. Either I am an object for the

Other, or, in order to escape the condition of being an object, I attempt to apprehend the Other as an object and thereby to re-apprehend myself as a free subject. Either I am a slave, or I am a master. Therefore 'conflict is the original meaning of being-for-others'. (*Ibid.,* p. 364)

Sartre's discussion is of great value insofar as it shows how the master-slave relation can be given a much wider application. In this sense it can much more plausibly be maintained that the attempt by each self to enslave the other is the permanent and necessary structure of self-consciousness. Certainly 'enslavement' in this sense, reduction of the other to an object, is a familiar aspect of human relations (we might refer again to the work of the existential psychiatrists to bear this out). Sartre's own argument that it is inevitable and inescapable simply begs the question; if we once grant the initial premise, that I can know another only as an object, then of course everything else follows. But we are still left with the problem of what *Hegel* really means. Once again, how can he apparently argue that the opposition of master and slave is a necessary condition of self-consciousness, and yet also claim that it can be historically surpassed?

4. The short answer, of course, is that he cannot – and that, insofar as he attempts to do so, he is confused and inconsistent. A more helpful and illuminating response, however, is to try to distinguish, within Hegel's account, between what he has shown to be the necessary requirements of self-consciousness, and the particular form which these may assume in historically specific societies. This is a distinction which Hegel himself has failed to make with sufficient clarity, but if we make it now it will enable us to make much better sense of his account.

In the first category, we can list the following necessary requirements of self-consciousness.

(i) *Recognition.* 'Self-consciousness exists in and for itself . . . only by being recognized.' This we have explained already.

(ii) *Freedom.* It is only by acting and being recognized as an autonomous and independent agent that man differentiates himself from objects in the natural world. To the extent that he acts freely, he is a person rather than a thing. The willingness to risk one's own life and that of others is apparently regarded by Hegel as the extreme demonstration of such freedom, a demonstration that man is not fettered to his corporeal existence but is willing to sacrifice it for an ideal.

(iii) *Work.* By working on the world, a man gives his own individuality an external, objective and enduring form. This is by far the most important point to emerge from the 'Master and Slave' section; it is indeed a turning-point in this section and in the *Phenomenology* as a whole — the recognition that self-consciousness requires not just that a man gets to know himself, but that he actively *produces* himself. Self-consciousness becomes self-realisation. This is a theme which runs right through the *Phenomenology*. It greatly influenced Marx, who says, with considerable justification:

> 'The outstanding achievement of Hegel's *Phenomenology* . . . is . . . that Hegel grasps the self-creation of man as a process, . . . and that he therefore grasps the nature of *labour*, and conceives objective man (true, because real man) as the result of his *own labour*.' (Karl Marx: 'Critique of Hegel's Dialectic and General Philosophy', in *Economic and Philosophical Manuscripts* p. 202)

The idea is most clearly expressed in the following passage from Hegel's *Lectures on Aesthetics*:

> 'Man is realised for himself by practical activity, inasmuch as he has the impulse, in the medium which is directly given to him, to produce himself, and therein at the same time to recognise himself. This purpose he achieves by the modification of external things upon which he impresses the seal of his inner being, and then finds repeated in them his own characteristics. Man does this in order as a free subject to strip the outer world of its stubborn foreignness, and to enjoy in the shape and fashion of things a mere external reality of himself. Even the child's first impulse involves this practical modification of external things. A boy throws stones into the river, and then stands admiring the circles that trace themselves on the water, as an effect in which he attains the sight of something of his own doing.' (Hegel: *On Art, Religion, Philosophy,* p. 58)

(iv) *Discipline.* This requirement is subsidiary to the previous one. Work requires the subjugation of self-will to external rules and standards. We can illustrate this by reference to the arts. 'Free self-expression', if this means simply the uncontrolled expression of immediate impulses, actually expresses nothing, let alone a 'self'. Genuine self-realisation through artistic work, and through work generally, requires the activity of forming and shaping, responding to the nature of the material, drawing on the accumulated experience of a tradition, satisfying given needs, and so on.

(v) With work and discipline, Hegel links the necessity of having been in *fear for one's life*. His reasoning seems to be that, unless one has vividly experienced the possibility of one's own death, one is not fully self-aware. Consciousness of myself as an independent self requires that I should have conceived of a world going on without me. This is true enough, I suppose; it takes time for a child to come to this realisation, and his doing so marks a stage in his developing self-awareness. But Hegel exaggerates when he implies that one must literally have been in mortal danger. This last requirement is the least interesting member of the list, and I shall conveniently forget about it.

Recognition, freedom, work and discipline are, then, features of human experience which are necessary for the achievement of a full self-consciousness. To be properly and universally realised, they require the existence of a free society in which everyone is recognised as a person, and in which all men work freely, serving not the needs of an individual master but the needs of the whole community, and subject only to the discipline of reason. To anticipate for a moment, such a society is described by Hegel at a later stage in the *Phenemenology* (pp. 374-8) and explicitly presented as a resolution of the contradic tions encountered in 'Self-consciousness'. Here, in the 'Master and Slave' section, Hegel has shown that these four requirements are necessary conditions of any fully-realized self-consciousness. But he has also shown that, in the absence of a free society, they are not found together in the experience of the individual, but are separated and attached to distinct social roles. Where the prevailing social relations are those of domination and submission, the master achieves recognition and freedom, whilst the slave experiences work and discipline. The self-realisation of each is therefore partial and incomplete.

To the 'theoretical abstraction' described in 'Consciousness' – the separation of moments from the totality – there here corresponds an 'abstraction in practice'. The abstraction of particular from universal, appearance from reality, etc., is of purely theoretical significance. The separation of the various aspects of self-realisation, on the other hand, is *lived*; in an unfree society, it is experienced as fragmentation, absence of fulfilment, loss of identity. And in distinguishing between the 'abstraction of concepts' on the one hand, and the 'fragmentation of experience' on the other, I am not simply contrasting them. For Hegel they are connected, the one is rooted in the other. In the 'Master and Slave' section we discover that problems of theory involve also problems of practice, of social relations and of historical change.

5. The above re-interpretation of Hegel does help to make his account more consistent, more plausible, and more useful. But it cannot, in all

honesty, be presented straightforwardly as 'what Hegel really meant'. I have suggested that self-consciousness can be seen as partial and incomplete *because of* the existence of domination and oppression. This means assuming the existence of the master-slave relation, and using it to explain the failure of self-consciousness. But there can be no doubt that Hegel sees himself as doing the opposite; the master-slave relation is, for him, not the explanation, but what is being explained. He is offering an answer to the question 'How does the master-slave relation come about?' – namely: 'It comes into existence as an initial stage in men's struggle to achieve self-consciousness and recognition.' And this has often been seen as the most objectionable feature of Hegel's account, especially from a Marxist point of view. He sees the master-slave relation primarily as a relation between *consciousnesses.* He ignores the material reality of oppression. Quite obviously, oppressive social relations cannot be adquately explained unless they are seen as rooted in the *physical domination* of some men by others. Less obviously but more importantly, Hegel sees conflict as a struggle for recognition between competing consciousnesses, and thereby ignores its foundation in the relations of *material production,* that is, in the ways in which men are related within a society organised for the satisfaction of *physical needs.* We are here entering on the question of Hegel's idealism, a topic which must now be reserved for further discussion in a later chapter.

A similar criticism might be brought against Hegel's account of work. In describing work as the means by which the slave achieves self-realisation, Hegel might be accused of considering only the *idea* of work, its ideal character, and ignoring its real nature in the material world, where it is likely to be stultifying and oppressive – especially if one is a slave, or even a wage-slave. This criticism would be less justified. We must not be misled by the fact that the 'Master and Slave' section ends with the 'turning of the tables' – the assertion that it is not the master but the slave who, because he works, is capable of self-realisation. For Hegel's final judgment is, as we have seen, that *neither* the master *nor* the slave is fully capable of self-realisation, since the experience of self-consciousness is fragmented and divided between them. This is not spelt out, however, until the beginning of the next section – 'Stoicism, Scepticism and the Unhappy Consciousness'. There Hegel says:

'The repressed and subordinated type of consciousness [i.e. the slave] . . . becomes, in the formative activity of work, an object to itself, in the sense that the form, given to the thing when shaped and moulded, is his object; he sees in the master, at the same time, being-for-itself as a real mode of consciousness. But the subservient consciousness as such finds *these two moments fall apart* – the moment of itself as independent object, and the moment of this object as a mode of consciousness, and so its own proper reality.' (p. 242 – my italics)

In other words, the slave objectifies himself, but does not recognize himself in his object, because he is not himself recognized as a free and independent consciousness.

6. It is important, then, to read this next section as a direct continuation of the 'Master and Slave' section. It makes explicit the inadequacies of self-consciousness in both master and slave, and describes various kinds of experience in which both of them will typically compensate for their failure to achieve full self-realisation in the real world by retreating into an inner world of *pure thought.*

Here is Hegel's explanation of why, in the activity of thinking, consciousness is free and conscious of itself as independent:

'For thinking, the object does not proceed by way of representations or figures, but of *concepts,* i.e. of a differentiated being-in-itself which, being an immediate content of consciousness, is nothing distinct from it. What is represented, shaped, and existent as such, has the form of being something other than consciousness. A concept is likewise something existent, . . . but insofar as this content is at the same time a conceptually constituted content, consciousness remains immediately aware within itself of its unity with this determinate existent . . . . In thinking, I am free, because I am not in an other, but remain simply and solely in touch with myself; . . . my procedure in dealing with concepts is a process within myself.' (p. 243)

This passage is particularly significant because it can be read as a statement of one of the main themes of the *Phenomenology,* and one which we encountered in 'Consciousness' – that, in bringing things under concepts, consciousness makes them its own and is at home in them. But we then have to reckon with the fact that, in the present section, Hegel criticises the standpoint which he is considering and shows it to be inadequate. His criticisms will therefore help to clarify his own position and the way in which it differs from the attitude being considered here.

This attitude of retreat from the real world into the world of thought is labelled 'Stoicism', for in the philosophy of the Stoics, as it existed in the Hellenistic world and in the Roman empire, such an attitude became the ideology of a historical epoch. Hegel's characterisation of it brings out clearly its relationship to the experience of the master and of the slave:

'The essence of this consciousness is to be free, on the throne as well as in fetters, throughout all the dependence that attaches to individual existence, and to maintain that stolid lifeless unconcern which persistently withdraws from the movement of existence, from effective activity as well as from passive endurance, into the simple essentiality of thought.' (p. 244)

The aim of such an attitude is to achieve freedom and self-possession by making itself immune to the hindrances and restrictions of the external world. But in fact it achieves the opposite. It does so, because the world of thought is regarded as entirely separate from the real world. Consequently:

'. . . by the way in which the concept as an abstraction cuts itself off from the multiplicity of things, the concept has *no content in itself*'. (p. 245)

The content of thought consequently has to be provided from the external world, as something simply *given.* The effect of setting the external world in opposition to the world of thought is therefore to exaggerate, rather than to diminish, the dependence of consciousness on something alien and external.

Hegel's own position is often identified with the sort of position here described. The *Phenomenology*, ending as it does with the 'Absolute Knowledge' of the philosopher, might seem to present the attitude of pure thought as that which alone overcomes the contradictions of all the previous modes of experience. Now it may be that Hegel can, in the end, be criticised for not differentiating his own position sufficiently from the attitude of retreat into pure thought; but it is certain that he would want to distinguish them. The attitude of Stoicism treats thought as an *abstraction,* set in *opposition* to reality. For Hegel himself, on the other hand, the statement 'In thinking I am free' means something different — not that I retreat into a realm of concepts, but that by the use of concepts I shape reality (in both theory and practice), so that the real world thereby becomes comprehensible and ceases to be something alien and hostile.

Once again, then, the term 'abstraction' conveys the nature of Hegel's critique. Stoicism becomes incoherent and contradictory because it isolates thought from reality instead of seeing them as necessarily inter-connected. And, as in the 'Master and Slave' section, the abstraction actually manifests itself in practice and in history. In a divided and oppressive society, the realm of thought is *experienced* as a retreat from the real world. Stoicism is a historical phenomenon, 'which can come on the scene as a general form of the world's spirit only in a time of universal fear and bondage, a time, too, when mental cultivation is universal, and has elevated culture to the level of thought' (p. 245).

7. The same is true of the next form of consciousness, 'Scepticism'. As a historical phenomenon, it too was one of the philosophies of the Hellenistic and Roman world. Hegel sees it as a response to the failure of Stoicism. The attitude of pure thought finds itself all the more dependent on an external content. Scepticism is accordingly the explicit negation of all the external content of thought. It proclaims the deceptive and contradictory nature of the evidence of the senses, of all empirical knowledge, all moral principles, etc. In so doing, it supposes that it is freed from all dependence on the outer world which Stoicism had to take as 'given'.

Like Stoicism, the attitude of Scepticism bears a certain resemblance to Hegel's own position. His procedure in the *Phenomenology* has been to criticise a succession of forms of thought and experience, and show each to be, by itself, untenable. He emphasises the resemblance between this and Scepticism in his description of the latter. Scepticism

'. . . shows the dialectic movement, which is sense-certainty, perception, and understanding. It shows too the unessentiality of that which holds good in the relation of master and servant . . . . Dialectic as a negative process, taken immediately as it stands, appears to consciousness in the first instance as something at the mercy of which it is, and which does not exist through consciousness itself. In Scepticism, on the other hand, this negative process is a moment of self-consciousness . . . Consciousness itself is thorough-going dialectical restlessness, this melee of presentations derived from sense and thought, whose differences collapse into oneness, and whose identity is similarly resolved and dissolved.' (pp. 247-9).

Also like Stoicism, however, Scepticism is an abstraction. Stoicism isolates the moment of pure thought. Scepticism isolates the moment of pure negativity. Hegel has already, in the Introduction, distinguished his own position from this purely negative scepticism:

'. . . the exposition of untrue consciousness in its untruth is not a merely negative process. Such a one-sided view of it is what the natural consciousness generally adopts; and a knowledge which makes this one-sidedness its essence is one of these shapes assumed by incomplete consciousness which falls into the course of the inquiry itself and will come before us there. For this view is scepticism, which always sees in the result only pure nothingness, and abstracts from the fact that this nothing is determinate, is the nothing of *that out of which* it comes as a result.' (p. 137).

This abstract negativity of Scepticism brings it into contradiction with itself. It supposes itself to occupy a secure position from which it can look down on the flux and confusion of all fallacious beliefs and experiences. But since it is pure negativity, and refuses to acknowledge the positivity of negation, it cannot provide itself with any positive position to occupy. It must apply its scepticism to itself, and assume that its own ideas are as fallacious and confused as any others. And yet in practice, of course, it can never do this:

'It announces the nullity of seeing, hearing, and so on, yet *itself* sees and hears. It proclaims the nothingness of essential ethical principles, and makes those very truths the sinews of its own conduct. Its deeds and its words belie each other continually . . .' (p. 250).

Although Hegel, in this section, has ancient scepticism mainly in mind, his remarks apply equally to a modern sceptic like Hume, who, when he is engaged in philosophy, is 'ready to reject all belief and reasoning', but, when he leaves such speculations in order to dine, play a game of back-gammon, and converse and be merry with his friends, finds himself 'absolutely and necessarily determined to live, and talk, and act like other people in the common affairs of life.'[5] Hegel's criticism must indeed apply to any attitude of all-embracing scepticism, for such scepticism can never, in the last resort, take itself seriously; its deeds always belie its words.

8. 'The Unhappy Consciousness' is Hegel's label for the consciousness which becomes explicitly aware of this division within itself. It is a divided self, not just in the sense of being a split personality in the

'Jekyll and Hyde' manner. Being *conscious* of its divided nature, it is a division within a unity. Consciousness identifies itself with one side of the split, but regards the other half as *both* a part of itself yet *also* alienated from itself. The division is therefore experienced *as* a division, and as the absence of a desired integrity. It is, in fact, a consciousness not just of the division implicit in Scepticism, but of that fundamental split in experience which stems from the master-slave relation:

> '. . . the duplication which previously was divided between two individuals, the master and the slave, is concentrated into one.' (p. 251).

So, to reiterate: the whole of 'Stoicism, Scepticism and the Unhappy Consciousness' should be read as a continuation of the 'Master and Slave' section, in order to arrive at a proper understanding of the latter and, in particular, to avoid the 'happy ending' interpretation of it.

Hegel's description of the Unhappy Consciousness is full of allusions to the doctrines and practices of Christianity, and this form of consciousness is, in its general character, a typically religious attitude. Being conscious of its division between an ever-changing identity and an unchanging one, it identifies its own experience with the former, which it regards as the false self, and projects the true self, the simple and unchanging self to which it aspires, into another world, a remote 'beyond'. Herein lies the substance of Hegel's critique. The religious consciousness is unsatisfactory just insofar as it fails to recognise, in its 'other world', the externalisation of its own self. We can see in 'The Unhappy Consciousness' a part of the *Phenomenology* which most obviously inspired Hegel's atheistic successors such as Feuerbach and Marx.

This is not to say that Hegel's view of religion is purely negative. He sees it as having a positive symbolic function. This aspect is emphasised more strongly in the later section on 'Religion', but in a passage in the present section Hegel alludes to the doctrine of the Trinity as a symbolic representation of the possible relationships between the changeable self and the unchangeableness to which it aspires (p. 253). God as Father represents the unchangeable as a remote 'beyond', an 'alien, external Being'; God as Son represents the possibility that the unchangeable can nevertheless become incarnate in an individual human life; and accordingly the doctrine of the Holy Spirit holds out the hope that the individual, the Unhappy Consciousness, may aspire to reconciliation with the unchangeable. Thus the ideas of the Incarnation and the Atonement represent to the Unhappy Consciousness the possibility of escaping from its divided condition; but at the same time this healing of the division is still represented in an alien and external form. Indeed, just because the figure of Christ represents the union of the present and the beyond in *another human individual*, this union is all the more remote. Instead of being a permanent human possibility, it is reduced to the status of a contingent historical event; 'it becomes a thing of the past, something that has been somewhere far away, and absolutely remote it remains' (p. 255). In this way the overcoming of alienation retains, within religion, its alienated form.

The aim of the Unhappy Consciousness is to destroy its own individuality, which it sees as a false self, in order to unite itself with the true and unchangeable. Hegel's critique then takes the form of asserting that any such attempt is self-defeating. The true self is to be found *within* the individual, not in a remote other world; it is implicit within the false self, not something totally separate from it. Consequently, in all its attempts to escape from itself and be reconciled with the unchangeable, consciousness finds only its own self. It cannot destroy its empirical self, since all the activities by which it attempts to do so are themselves the achievements of this same empirical self and therefore simply re-affirm it. Every success is a success on the part of the false, empirical self, and therefore a failure. The whole endeavour is 'a struggle against an enemy, victory over whom really means being worsted' (p. 252).

After stating this critique in general terms (pp. 252-3), Hegel applies it to three specific ways in which the Unhappy Consciousness tries to reconcile itself with the unchangeable:

(i) *Inner feeling* (pp. 256^{15}-259^4): Consciousness tries to unite itself with the unchangeable through mystical experience or through religious worship and ritual. But just because it is confined to pure feeling rather than conceptual thought, it can never find anything except subjective states of feeling, that is, states of its own self.

(ii) *Work* (pp. 259^5-262^{28}): Consciousness sees its work not as self-objectification, but as the confirmation of its own disunity. It ascribes every success not to itself but to the unchangeable, that is, to God as the author of the world on which it works and the provider of the talents which it employs. By this means it aims to become simply the instrument of the unchangeable and so achieve unity with it. But it cannot consistently maintain this attitude. It cannot help finding fulfilment in work, it cannot help getting a sense of satisfaction from it, even from the very act of renouncing its satisfaction. Consequently its activity remains an affirmation of its empirical self.

(iii) *Self-denial* (pp. 262^{29}-267^{32}): The final expedient must therefore consist in an explicit activity of self-negation. This at first takes the form of asceticism. But asceticism has its familiar ambiguity. The more one aims at mortification of the flesh, the more one becomes obsessed with it. As Hegel puts it, the animal functions, 'instead of being performed unconsciously and naturally as something which is of no significance in itself', become 'an object of strenuous concern and serious occupation' (p. 263). Instead of escaping from the individual self, one is preoccupied with it. The only way in which consciousness can effectively annihilate itself is by shedding its own responsibility for doing so, and by casting it on to another, the 'mediator' — that is, the priest, who takes upon himself the task of bringing the individual consciousness into relation with the unchangeable. Consciousness thereby eleminates the very fact of its own agency. It participates in a meaningless ritual conducted in a language it does not understand; its 'self-denial' takes the form of paying tithes and performing penances imposed by the priest. From none of this can it obtain any fulfilment or satisfaction. But the final irony is this: having finally succeeded in reducing itself to nothing, the Unhappy Consciousness is promised by the priest the reward of fulfilment in another world; and in this promise is contained the truth that fulfilment and self-realisation *is* to be found by consciousness *as an individual*.

This final dialectical twist is intended as the transition to a discussion of Idealism and to the recognition that 'Reason. . . is all reality'. The transition seems entirely arbitrary. It is a mere assertion on Hegel's part, and this assertion could have been made at any point in the section. If the promise of an afterlife is an implicit recognition of the fact that consciousness must find in itself the true reality, this is no more than Hegel has already said of, for example, the doctrine of the Incarnation. The arbitrariness of this transition matches the arbitrariness of the transition at the end of 'Consciousness' (to which it is intended to be directly parallel), and suggests that the transitions between the major sections are of a different order from those within the sections.

The real conclusion of 'The Unhappy Consciousness' however, is to be found not in the final sentence, but in the persistent theme of the whole section. This theme is the same one as emerged at the end of the 'Master and Slave' section — the claim that all human activity, and in particular all human work, is necessarily a means of self-realisation, albeit in distorted forms. This is not to be confused with a crudely egoistic theory of action. The suggestion is not that everyone always acts with a view to his own interests. It is that one's actions are always a confirmation of one's own identity. Insofar as we can link this idea at all with any more familiar philosophical theory, it would be with behaviourism. The similarities are to a certain extent explored in the later section 'Physiognomy and Phrenology'. Hegel says there, for example:

> 'The true being of a man is. . . his act. . . . The act does away with the inexpressibleness of what self-conscious individuality really "means"; in regard to such "meaning", individuality is endlessly determined and determinable. This false infinite, this endless determining, is abolished in the completed act. The act is something simply determinate. . .; it is murder, theft, a benefit, a deed of bravery, and so on, and what it *is* can be *said* of it. It *is* such and such, and its being is not merely a symbol, it is the fact itself. It *is* this, and the individual human *is* what the *act is*. In the simple fact that the act *is*, the individual is for others what he really is and with a certain general nature, and ceases to be merely something that is "meant" or "presumed" to be this or that. . . . When his performance and his inner possibility, capacity, or intention are opposed, the former *alone* is to be regarded as his true reality.' (pp. 349-350).

This might at first look like a straightforward behaviourism – 'a man is his act'. But this is too simple. Hegel is not denying the existence of the 'inner'. What he seems to be saying, rather, is that in some sense the merely inner is not *determinate*. I take him to mean something like the following. To have a sense of identity, to be aware of myself as a person, I must be able to form some idea of *who* or *what* I am. It must be possible for me to regard the various aspects of myself as forming some kind of coherent unity, making me this kind of person rather than that. Now, at the level of my thoughts and intentions, this cannot be done. My thoughts and intentions are limitlessly redescribable, open to innumerable interpretations. I may assure myself, and others, that 'this is what I am *really* like' – for example that, despite my actions, I am not really a coward, that my apparently cowardly acts are not really typical of me but are just unfortunate lapses, that my real capacities and intentions are quite other, etc. Now, the point is not that these assertions are necessarily false, but that, at this level, there is *no way of*

63

distinguishing true from false, no way in which even I myself can distinguish my own self-deception from reality. The assertion that I am not really a coward can be regarded as objective only if it is, literally, *made* objective, objectified in my acts. This is not to deny that my acts may give a misleading impression of what I really am. But to correct that impression is to *re-characterise the acts*, to show, for example, that when seen in the context of certain other acts they take on a new aspect.

Two further points must be added to complete our interpretation of Hegel's position:

(i) Productive work has a special status as a means of self-realisation, because it possesses in a special degree the relevant features of action. Through productive work the individual is objectified, quite literally, in an *object*, in the product of his work. Though he cannot contemplate his own acts in the way that others can contemplate them, he can contemplate his product as an expression of his identity. And this is connnected with the fact that, as Hegel has stressed, the product has a certain *permanence*.

(ii) Hegel's assertions, in the section on the Unhappy Consciousness, that one cannot help getting satisfaction and fulfilment from one's work, have to be understood in this context. Of course asceticism and self-denial are possible in the sense that one can deprive oneself of material pleasures of one sort or another. What one cannot do, according to Hegel, is deliberately engage in activity to eliminate one's own identity. In *this* sense, self-denial is impossible; any activity, even of this kind, is an expression and objectification of one's identity. Again, within the master-slave relation, the slave's work may produce for him only a fragmented and alienated identity. But we can understand such work as alienation only if we also recognise that it is implicitly self-objectification.

9. Hegel's treatment of 'Self-consciousness' differs in some ways from his treatment of 'Consciousness', as well as from the method laid down in the Introduction. But first we should note the continuities. The treatment remains dialectical — that is to say, it consists in demonstrating the instability of *abstractions*, of concepts which are incomplete in themselves and require to be taken as moments in a totality. I have emphasised this already in the present chapter and do not need to repeat the instances. Secondly, the overall project is still the one which was set out in the Introduction: to bridge the gap between subject and object. This brings us to the first of the innovations. The attempt in

this section has been to bridge the gap not from the side of the object, but from the side of the subject. This is important. For Hegel, the subject-object dichotomy is to be overcome not simply by developing our conception of the object until it is reducible to a state of the subject (as in subjective idealism). Not only our conception of the object, but also our conception of the subject, has to be developed and extended.

Since consciousness here has *itself* for its object, the method of criticism cannot be the same as it was in the 'Consciousness' section. There, it will be remembered, the critique proceeded by revealing contradictions between the conception which consciousness has of its *object* and the conception it has of itself; clearly this is no longer possible when the object *is* the self. Hegel still proceeds by setting up a form of consciousness and then revealing contradictions within it, but the contradictions must now be of a different sort. Of *what* sort, exactly? Before answering this question, we should note a second important innovation in the 'Self-consciousness' section.

In 'Consciousness', we were dealing entirely with forms of thought. Here, as I have repeatedly stressed, we are dealing also with forms of *action*. This is not a mere change of subject-matter. Hegel has actually *shown* that self-consciousness *cannot* be simply a form of thought. One can be conscious of one's identity only if one is also an agent. This is the most important respect in which the conception of the subject has been extended: the subject is not just a thinker, but is active in the world.

Given that the stages of 'Self-consciousness' are forms of action, we can now see the nature of the contradictions which arise within them. They are contradictions between the *intention* and the *result* of the activity. For example, the master intends, by defeating the slave, to obtain recognition from him; but just because the slave is made into an instrument of the master's will, he cannot provide the master with objective confirmation of his identity. The Stoic attempts to free himself from the external world by withdrawing into the world of thought, but just for that reason he becomes all the more dependent on the external world. The Unhappy Consciousness aims to eliminate his empirical self, but all his attempts to do so serve only to confirm that self. Thus, with the focus on action, Hegel's method has been significantly modified.

The emphasis on action brings with it two other innovations: consciousness becomes *social*, and it becomes *historical*. Both these innovations, however, are as yet incomplete. We have seen that self-consciousness requires the existence of another self-consciousness. But we have not yet arrived at the conception of a genuinely social existence, where men mutually recognise one another and are recognised. The social relations described here are ones which continue to isolate men from one another and set them against one another. Moreover, Hegel is still concerned with the individual consciousness rather than with the form of society as such. And for that reason, his treatment is not yet genuinely historical. He is concerned with the form that self-consciousness may take, given a context of certain kinds of social relations, as they are to be found in certain periods of human history. But the historical aspect is still in the background. In the next two chapters we shall see how the focus shifts again, to become genuinely social and genuinely historical.

[1] It is considered as such by Sartre in *Being and Nothingness* Pt. III Ch. I, Section III.

[2] R. D. Laing, *The Divided Self* and *Self and Others*; R. D. Laing and A. Esterson, *Sanity, Madness and the Family*. Part II of *Self and Others*, in particular, can be read as a valuable elaboration of Hegel's concept of 'recognition'.

[3] They have only recently been translated, and are to be found in *Hegel's Philosophy of Mind*, trans. William Wallace and A. V. Miller.

[4] Jean-Paul Sartre, *Being and Nothingness*; pp. 235-244 deal specifically with Hegel, but the whole of Part III, and especially ch. 1, exhibits Sartre's interpretation of and reaction to Hegel's 'Master and Slave'.

[5] David Hume: *A Treatise of Human Nature* Book I, Part IV, Section VII.

4

REASON AND ETHICS

1. 'Reason', then, is consciousness which *knows itself to be all reality*. What does Hegel means by this phrase? One answer would be to say that the whole of the *Phenomenology* is intended as an elaboration of it. But this, though true, is not very helpful. A more specific explanation is given in the introductory section to 'Reason', which Hegel entitles 'Certainty and Truth of Reason'. The idea that 'reason is the conscious certainty of being all reality' is there seen to have two aspects.

(a) In the first place, it apparently indicates a confidence that the world is rational and can be rationally understood. There are no incomprehensible mysteries, nothing that is in principle beyond the reach of rational understanding. Hegel says of this attitude:

'To it, looking at itself in this way, it seems as if now, for the first time, the world had come into being. . . . . It discovers the world as its own new and real world, which in its permanence possesses an interest for it, just as previously [for the Unhappy Consciousness] the interest lay only in its transitoriness.' (p. 273).

This description is elaborated in more concrete historical terms in the following passage from the *Philosophy of History*:

'Spirit has now advanced to the level of thought. It involves the reconciliation [of self and object] in the purest essence, challenging the external world to exhibit the same reason which the subject possesses. Spirit perceives that nature, the world, must also be an embodiment of reason, for God created it on principles of reason. An interest in the observation and comprehension of the present world became universal. . . . Experimental science became the science of the world, for experimental science involves on the one hand the observation of phenomena, on the other hand also the discovery of the law, the essential being, the hidden force that causes those phenomena. . . . It seemed to men as if God had but just created the moon and stars, plants and animals, as if the laws of the universe were now established for the first time. For only then did they feel a real interest in the universe when they recognized their own reason in the reason which pervades it. The human eye became clear, perception quick, thought active and interpretative. The discovery of the laws of nature enabled men to contend against the monstrous superstition of the time, as also against all notions of mighty alien powers which magic alone could conquer. . . . The independent authority of the subject was maintained against belief founded on authority, and the laws of nature were recognized as the only bond connecting phenomena with phenomena. Thus all miracles were disallowed, for nature is a system of known and recognized laws. Man is at home in it, and that only passes for truth in which he finds himself at home; he is free through the knowledge of nature. Nor was thought less vigorously directed to the spiritual side of things. Right and morality came to be looked upon as having their foundation in the actual present will of man, whereas formerly it was referred only to the command of God enjoined from without.' (*Philosophy of History* pp. 439. In this quotation I have also drawn on Carl J. Friedrich's translation in his collection *The Philosophy of Hegel* pp. 142-4.)

Hegel is here describing the re-awakening of science and philosophy in post-Renaissance and post-Reformation Europe, and the remarks in the *Phenomenology* must be intended to have the same reference. Accordingly, the subsequent sections of 'Reason' are devoted to various instances of this rational thought — first to examples of reason in its theoretical application, in the form of various scientific ideas and theories (pp. 281-372), and then to examples of practical reason, in the form of attempts to establish a rational basis for human action (pp. 373-453). All these are to be seen as attempts to formulate theoretical and practical *laws*; for in formulating laws, consciousness is no longer a mere passive receiver of data, but is conscious of itself as the activity of reason, and conscious of the world as the embodiment of reason.

(b) In this introductory section, however, Hegel is primarily concerned not with these specific ways in which 'reason knows itself to be all reality', but with the philosophical expression of this principle. To assert that thought is all reality is, apparently, to adhere to the philosophical position of *Idealism*. But Hegel considers that there are serious defects in previous versions of Idealism, and the remainder of this introductory section is devoted to pointing them out. The criticisms appeared to be directed mainly against the idealism of Kant and Fichte. They are set out in complex fashion, but they reduce to the following:

(i) At this stage in the *Phenomenology*, Idealism has emerged from the development of the previous modes of thought, and this is its justification. What Hegel terms the 'abstract' form of idealism, on the other hand, appeals to a supposed intuitive certainty – Kant's 'All my representations are mine', Fichte's 'I am I'. These bare assertions could, however, be opposed with the equally intuitive certainties that all my representations have an object, that 'I' am confronted with a 'not-I'. This confrontation of subject and object is a feature of the forms of consciousness dealt with earlier in the *Phenomenology* – sense-certainty, perception and understanding. Hegel claims to have shown how these lead into Idealism, which is therefore, for him, effectively established and not a mere assertion (pp. 273-5).

(ii) With Kant and Fichte the idealist thesis is made to rest on the *formal* features of consciousness – its unity, its spatio-temporal structure, etc. But this form must be imposed on a *content*, and if one goes on to enquire about the nature and origin of this content, no answer can be given from within Kant's or Fichte's idealism. They resort to the notion of something *external* to consciousness which provides it with its content. Kant talks in terms of 'sensibility', or again of the 'thing-in-itself'; Fichte speaks of an 'alien impact' (pp. 279-280). Thus they are idealists in respect of the form of consciousness, but not in respect of its content. Their idealism is 'a one-sided, unsound idealism which lets this unity [of thought and being] appear on one side as consciousness, with a reality *in itself* over against it on the other' (p. 276).

(iii) The same inadequacy is apparent in Kant's deduction of the particular categories. By appealing to the fact that 'all my representations are mine', Kant attempts to establish idealism in the form of the doctrine of the synthetic unity of apperception, the doctrine that all my representations have to be synthesised within the unity of a single self-consciousness. Hegel refers to this 'unity of apperception' as 'the Category bare and simple' (p. 276). But, he adds, if the unity of apperception is to have a content it must have variety and differentiation within it, and Kant must therefore effect a transition from 'the

Category bare and simple' to a *plurality* of categories. This he does, according to Hegel, in a purely arbitrary manner:

> 'But to pick up the various categories again in any sort of way as a kind of happy find, hit upon, e.g. in the different judgments, and then to be content so to accept them, must really be regarded as an outrage on scientific thinking.' (p. 277)

Hegel has in mind the so-called 'Metaphysical Deduction', in which Kant suggests that the table of the various forms of judgments provides a definitive list of the categories. Hegel's point once again is that, instead of letting the categories emerge from a necessary process of development (as Hegel himself claims to do), Kant has recourse to external considerations; the list of categories is simply empirically given. (Such a criticism would, however, be less applicable to Kant's Transcendental Deduction, to which Hegel makes no reference.)

2. I shall not say much about the various stages of 'Reason'. It has three main sub-divisions, the first of these ('Observational Reason') being concerned with theoretical reason and the other two with practical reason. 'Observational Reason' is further divided into three sections. The first, 'Observation of Nature', is tough going indeed, and its contributions to the philosophy of the natural sciences can hardly be said to repay the effort required to look for them. The second section, 'Observation of Self-consciousness. . .', is more amenable. It deals with logical and psychological laws, and contains the very Sartrean claim that a state of the world can be said to determine the behaviour of an individual only insofar as it is comprehended by him as *his* world and endowed by him with a meaning. Having dealt first with 'observation of nature' and secondly with 'observation of self-consciousness', Hegel then, in the third section, turns to the relation between nature and self-consciousness – that is, the relation between body and mind, on which he has some good things to say, though formulated in terms of the now-forgotten 'sciences' of physiognomy and phrenology.

The stages of practical reason are then prefaced by another very important introductory section (pp. 374-382), to which I shall devote most of the remainder of this chapter.

3. The introductory section is headed 'Self-realisation of Rational Self-consciousness' and the term 'self-realisation' is important. The previous section was concerned with the idea of an identity between mind and a physical thing. The truth which Hegel elicits from this

discussion is that self-consciousness must indeed have an objective existence in the external world — not, however, as mere inert matter (e.g. the shape of the skull, as phrenology would have it). Rather, it must objectify itself through its own activity, realise itself in the world.

This returns us to the theme of 'Self-consciousness', especially in the 'Master and Slave' section, and Hegel now explicitly takes up that theme. Just as 'Observational Reason' has repeated at a higher level the movement of 'Consciousness', so the sections to follow will continue the process of 'Self-consciousness' — the search for recognition, the attempt to 'bring forth one's reality in an "other" '. The end of this process and the culmination of these stages will be a situation of universal mutual recognition. This is the situation which we mentioned in our previous chapter as the resolution of the contradictions in the master-slave relation.

In order to follow Hegel's remarks here, it is essential to bear in mind the structure of this part of the *Phenomenology*:

V. *Reason*
    V.A. Observational Reason
    V.B. Self-realisation of Rational Self-consciousness
    V.C. Individuality which takes itself to be real in and for itself.

VI. *Spirit*
    VI.A. Objective Spirit: Ethics (Sittlichkeit)
    VI.B. Self-estranged Spirit: Culture
    VI.C. Spirit certain of itself: Morality

The situation of universal recognition which Hegel at this point anticipates will finally be reached in the section called 'Spirit'. The German word translated as 'spirit' is 'Geist', which can also be translated as 'mind' and is the same word as appears in the title of the work — *Phänomenologie des Geistes*. Thus the whole of the *Phenomenology* is about 'spirit', but only in Part VI do we arrive at 'spirit' in its true sense, which is for Hegel, as we shall see, not an individual mind but a collective entity — the spirit of a people. The intervening stages leading up to 'Spirit' (i.e. the three sections of V.B. and the three sections of V.C.) are said by Hegel to be abstractions from Spirit, moments of it which 'break loose and appear as forms on their own account, but have in fact only existence and actuality when borne and supported by it' (p. 375). This will be explained later. But first, Hegel devotes the next few pages (pp. 375^{21}-378^{19}) to a further elaboration of the end result.

This situation of universal recognition is, he says, the realm of *ethics* — Sittlichkeit. The word is derived from 'Sitte', which means 'custom', and Hegel regards the derivation as important, for he interprets Sittlichkeit as the ordering of one's actions by reference to the *customs* and *laws* of a society. The laws are the objective aspect; they are independent of the individual, who observes them. But at the same time they are embodied in the actions of individuals, as customs, and in this aspect the individual does not regard them as external to him, but as his own being. They constitute his own individuality; he is what he is because he has absorbed and appropriated the ways of thinking and acting of the community in which he has grown up:[1]

> 'This ethical substance when taken in its abstract universality is . . . law . . . ; but just as much it is immediately actual self-consciousness, it is custom. The single individual conversely is only a "this", a given existent unit, in so far as he is aware of the universal consciousness as his own being in his own particular individuality, seeing that his action and existence are the universal custom.' (p. 376).

The same two aspects are reiterated in the next paragraph (376^{12-33}). The ethical realm is 'unchangeable simple thinghood', an objective entity to which individuals 'surrender and sacrifice their particular individuality', but it is also 'their soul and essence', it is 'the action of themselves as individuals, and is the work and product of their own activity.' Because it combines these two aspects, Hegel sees it as solving the problem of self-realisation. As members of a social order, men find themselves objectified in the laws and customs which transcend their own individuality (this was what the master lacked); but because all are free and are recognized as such, they experience the social order not as something alien but as the expression and product of their own individuality (this was what the slave lacked). In a free society there can be objectification without alienation, and so Hegel asserts that 'the notion of the realization of self-conscious reason . . . finds its complete reality in fulfilment in the life of a nation.'

As it resolves the problem of self-realisation, such a society also resolves the problem of work. Hegel emphasises that economic activity is by its very nature social. Even when a man is apparently working simply as an individual to satsify his own individual needs, his work depends for its success on the economic activities of innumerable other individuals. (This is true of any society based on the division of labour, i.e. any but the most primitive community; and it is true to an increasing degree as the division of labour increases. The 'self-made man' is a myth). Conversely, in working for himself each man is also working for others, just as they are working for him. But a society of universal recognition is one in which work is *consciously* social, and the individual worker finds himself confirmed in his own work and in the work of the community:

' . . . he performs the universal task as his *conscious* object. The whole becomes *in its entirety* his work, for which he sacrifices himself, and precisely by that means receives back his own self from it.' (p. 377).

Thus the worker here achieves that recognition which the slave was unable to obtain from his work, and finds his own identity reflected in others.

'I apprehend and see [in others] that they are in their own eyes only these independent beings just as I am. I see in their case the free unity with others in such wise that just as this unity exists through me, so it exists through the others too – I see them as myself, myself as them.' (p. 378).

Clearly this vision of unalienated labour and universal recognition must, no less than the more famous 'Master and Slave' section, have greatly influenced Marx's early writings.[2]

Finally Hegel appears to suggest that such a society solves not only the problems of self-realisation, of work and recognition, but also the problem of the basis of morality, for he adds:

'In a free nation, therefore, reason is in truth realized. . . . The wisest men of antiquity for that reason declared that wisdom and virtue consist in living in accordance with the customs of one's own nation.' (p. 378).

I shall return to this point later.

Before proceeding any further, I want to raise a general question about Hegel's discussion so far. Does his concept of Sittlichkeit assert a *universally valid* relation between any individual and his society, or does it represent a *particular historical phenomenon,* an ideal which may or may not be realised in particular societies? I pose this question because the most famous English statement of Hegelian ethics – Bradley's essay 'My Station and its Duties' – suggests the former interpretation. Bradley states that 'we have found self-realization, duty, and happiness . . . when we have found our station and its duties, our function as an organ in the social organism' (*Ethical Studies* p. 163); and he appears to mean that self-realization consists in performing the duties of one's station in the society in which one happens to find oneself, whatever that society may be. Hegel's own position is more complex. He would agree with Bradley that 'what we call an individual man is what he is because of and by virtue of community' (*Ethical Studies* p. 166). That is to say, 'the individual' is an abstraction, and all the distinctively human activities which an individual engages in, such as language and work, are necessarily social. But not every society allows for these activities to constitute genuine self-realisation. Hegel's claim is: 'In a *free nation* . . . reason is in truth realized'. And not every nation is a free nation. For Hegel, a free nation is one in which all men are free. This freedom he regards as being progressively realized in history. So the historical dimension *is* important for Hegel, in a way in which it is not for Bradley, and the role which he here ascribes to Sittlichkeit, to 'the customs and laws of a nation', is fully realized only in certain societies.

4. This is confirmed in the remaining pages of the present section (378^{20}-382^{36}), for Hegel now goes on to say:

'From this happy state, however, of having attained its identity and of living in it, self-consciousness, which in the first instance is only immediately and in principle spirit, has broken away . . .' (p. 378).

(He adds: '. . . or perhaps it has not yet attained it: for both can be said with equal truth.' This alternative formulation is explained shortly).

Hegel is further anticipating the course of the 'Spirit' section. The move is from the first section of 'Spirit' — Objective Spirit and Sittlichkeit — to the second section and the world of Self-estranged Spirit. And this represents, in historical terms, the breakdown of the ancient Greek world. Hegel, like many of his contemporaries, looked back with admiration to the Greek city-states, especially Athens. They represented for him a model of the ethical community, in which men find their identity immediately in the life of the society.[3] The disintegration of the city-state, however, leads to a privatised world in which men experience themselves as isolated individuals for whom society is something alien and external. This is the world, first, of the Hellenistic and Roman empires, and then of mediaeval Christian Europe.

Hegel's explanation of the breakdown of the Greek ethical world starts from the fact that the city-state is a *particular* community. In

Hegel's words, it is

'. . . an existent social order, and in consequence this universal mind is also an individualized mind. It is the totality of customs and laws of a particular people, a specifically determinate ethical substance.' (p. 378).

Hegel has in mind, I think, the way in which the growth of trade in the Greek world led to an increasing awareness of the diversity of customs between one society and another. This awareness is represented by the distinction made by many of the Sophists between 'convention' and 'nature': the inherited customs of a society are simply the conventions of that particular society, and are to be contrasted with what is right by nature (cf. *Philosophy of History,* pp. 265-271).

This leads to a change in the relation of the individual to his society. Formerly the individual had felt a 'solid imperturbable confidence' in the objective social order. He had identified himself with the practices of his society and had never regarded them as questionable; they were for him, as it were, part of the fabric of the universe. But when once he becomes aware of the diversity of social customs and hence recognises that those of his own society could be other than they are,

'. . . his naive confidence is lost. Isolated by himself, he is himself now the central essential reality . . . . The individual has thereby set himself over against the laws and customs.' (p. 379).

Referring again to the *Philosophy of History,* we can discover that Hegel regarded this tendency as personified in Socrates, who relentlessly questioned conventional morality, not because he was necessarily hostile to it but because he wanted men's actions to derive from their own rational understanding of what is right (Op. cit. pp. 269-270).

Hegel now explains his alternative formulation – that consciousness can also be regarded not as having broken away from, but as having *not yet attained* the condition of Sittlichkeit. This has again to be understood in terms of the structure of the *Phenomenology.* The reference is to the several forms of practical reason which are to be discussed in sections V.B. and V.C., immediately after this introductory section, and which lead up to 'Spirit'. Hegel thereby implies that these forms of consciousness can be historically located in the world of self-estrangement (i.e. in VI.B.). They are thus forms of individualism, forms of practical rationality characteristic of a world in which the individual is set over against society. The various attitudes adopted – those of pleasure, sentiment, virtue, etc. – are all abstractions from the ethics of the social world, and therefore find their truth only as moments of the latter. In this sense, Sittlichkeit is 'not yet attained'. I shall try to explain all this shortly.

After a further comparison of the two points of view, that of V.B-C and that of VI.B., Hegel completes his anticipatory survey of the stages of 'Spirit'. If Self-estranged Spirit has broken away from the realm of Sittlichkeit, what does it in turn lead up to? What is the social condition in which self-estrangement is eliminated? Here is Hegel's answer:

> 'In the former case [i.e. sections V.B-C] the goal which they attain is the *immediate* ethical substance; while, in the latter [i.e. section VI.B], the end is the *consciousness of* that substance, such a consciousness as knows the substance to be its own essential being; and to that extent this process would be the development of *morality,* a higher state or attitude than the former. But these modes at the same time constitute only one side of the development of morality, that, namely, which belongs to being-for-itself, or in which consciousness cancels its purposes; they do not constitute the side where morality arises out of the substance itself.' (p. 381 – my italics).

This raises problems. The clear implication of the first sentence is that the stage of 'Self-estranged Spirit' is to be succeeded by the stage of 'Morality', and 'Morality' is indeed the title of the third and final section of 'Spirit' (VI.C). So far, so good. Now Morality is said to be 'a higher state or attitude than the former'. Does this mean higher than VI.A (Sittlichkeit) or higher than VI.B (Self-estranged Spirit)? Either alternative is awkward. For, when we get to the section on 'Morality', we find there a discussion of Kantian moral theory. And the trouble is that Kantian morality is also one of the forms of moral individualism discussed in V.C. and therefore historically locatable in the Self-estranged World. Moreover, 'morality' (Moralität) is the term which Hegel regularly uses, in a general way, to indicate the individualist attitude which he contrasts with social 'ethics' (Sittlichkeit). (The terminology may be rather confused in the *Phenomenology,* but this distinction is quite clearly made in, for example, the *Philosophy of Right* and the *Philosophy of History*). Given Hegel's insistence that individualist moral attitudes are abstractions from Sittlichkeit and find their truth in the latter, this ought to mean that Sittlichkeit is a higher state or attitude than Moralität.

However, if we are not too preoccupied with labels, I think we can manage to extract a coherent doctrine from the passage. The original situation is one in which the individual identifies himself *immediately* with the laws and customs of his society; he does so because he has never questioned them. This is the condition which Hegel calls 'immediate ethical substance' and which he finds exemplified in the Greek world prior to the Sophists. It is therefore a necessary historical advance that individuals should detach themselves from this immediate identification with their society and should resolve to act solely on the basis of their own rational conviction. Their attempts to do this are expressed in familiar moral theories and attitudes such as hedonism, utilitarianism, the morality of sentiment, etc. The highest of these is Kantian morality. But they are all one-sided, just as 'immediate ethical substance' had been one-sided in the opposite respect. They all rest on the assumption that the individual can provide a morality out of his own private rationality, whereas in fact the concepts which they focus on – pleasure, virtue, conscientiousness, etc – derive from, and have their proper significance within, the shared practices of an ethical community. What is required is a synthesis of these two one-sided extremes, a synthesis in which the individual acts only on what he sees to be rational, but now recognises that reason is embodied in social practices. This could be described equally as a 'morality [which] arises out of the ethical substance itself' and as an ethics which is *conscious of itself*. It is a synthesis which Hegel regards as possible for the first time in the modern world.

5. Hegel has now to show, in the sections which follow, that these individualist moral attitudes do break down *because* they are individualist. He summarises them on the last of these introductory pages (p. 382), but the reference is too cryptic to be enlightening. I shall therefore look briefly, though not in detail, at the sections themselves.

It is essential to read Hegel's account of these stages in the light of the problems of objectification and recognition. Consciousness has not yet attained the experience of universal recognition in the ethical world. The forms of activity which it engages in are attempts at self-realisation, but they all contain that division which Hegel has previously ascribed to the slave (p. 374). On the one hand, consciousness acts on the world and objectifies itself, on the other, it sees itself reflected in other consciousnesses; but 'these two moments fall apart'. This split, between objectification and duplication, is what gives rise to the contradictions. Consciousness is confronted with an 'other' (i.e. another consciousness), and this 'other' has a two-fold character, as the *object* on which consciousness acts, and as the *mirror* in which consciousness recognises itself. The attitude of hedonism, for example, involves treating the other as something which exists simply to be enjoyed; but consciousness also sees itself reflected in the 'other', which it must regard as another consciousness seeking its own independent enjoyment and therefore as a rival, as something hostile and intractable. The 'other' thus acquires a contradictory character. Similarly when consciousness adopts the attitude of sentimentalism (the 'Law of the Heart') it treats the 'other' both as an object of sympathy and benevolence, and as an independent consciousness with its own sentiments, obeying the edicts of its own heart and therefore coming into conflict with the first consciousness.

All such forms of consciousness become self-contradictory because consciousness *first* sees itself as an individual seeking objectification, and then, as a *second* step, looks for the reflection of itself in others. It is in this respect that these attitudes are individualist. Consequently they find their true, non-contradictory form when they become modes of social life, activities which are recognised from the start to be social activities − when enjoyment is pursued by human beings acting in common, when the 'laws of the heart' become the laws and customs of a community, and so on.[4]

6. The divorce between the individual and the universal aspects of practical reason becomes most clearly apparent in Kant's concept of 'universalisability', which Hegel discusses in the section on 'Reason as Testing Laws' (V.C.c.). Hegel agrees with Kant that rational action must, in some sense, satisfy the requirement of universality. But the universality in question must be, not a hypothetical universalisability, but an *actual* universality, the universality of social laws and customs. The discussion in the *Phenomenology* is confused, and Hegel's criticisms of Kant are stated more clearly in the *Philosophy of Right* (para. 135) and elsewhere. However, the criticisms are the same in each case, and if one reads the version in the *Philosophy of Right* this can help one to understand what Hegel is saying in the *Phenomenology* version.

Hegel focuses on an example which Kant employs in the *Critique of Practical Reason* (27), of a man who is wondering whether to keep for himself a deposit entrusted to him by someone who has since died. Hegel's comment is:

'Suppose a deposit has been made over to me on trust, it is the property of another, and I recognise it because it is so, and remain immovable in this relation towards it. But if I keep the deposit for myself, then, according to the principle I use in testing laws — tautology — I undoubtedly do not commit a contradiction; for in that case I do not regard it any longer as the property of another. To keep anything which I do not look on as the property of some one else is perfectly consistent.' (p. 452-3).

Kant would now say that, if I *universalise* the maxim of my proposed action, then there would indeed be a contradiction. For if everyone aimed to increase his property by every means in his power, including treating other people's property as his own, then the institution of property would cease to exist. To this, however, Hegel replies that the non-existence of property does not, in itself, involve any contradiction at all (pp. 447-9). And he would make the same comment on any of Kant's examples. Kant says, for example, that if everyone made lying promises the institution of promising would cease to exist; Hegel's comment would be that no contradiction is involved in the non-existence of promising. And in general Hegel would say that if 'universalisability' is our only criterion for testing moral laws, then by this principle absolutely any action may be justified.

Hegel is not denying that the universalising of practical maxims may lead to contradictions. What he is saying, in criticism of Kant, is that no such universalised moral principle *by itself* involves a contradiction. It can come into contradiction only with *something else*, which must therefore be already presupposed. In the above example, if it is already presupposed that property ought to exist, that it is an institution which men need, etc., then of course this presupposition would contradict the principle that everyone should disregard other people's property rights. Only, the latter principle does not by itself involve any contradiction.

This distinction needs to be kept in mind when we consider attempts by recent philosophers to defend Kant. Marcus Singer, for instance, says: 'Hegel assumes that the categorical imperative is supposed to be applied in a vacuum — or in other words, is not to be applied to anything, with the possible exception of itself. . .'; and Singer then goes on to say that this is not Kant's intention, that the original maxim of the action provides the content to which the universalisability principle is applied and with which it can come into contradiction.[5] But this is exactly Hegel's point: something else, some requirement or principle or value or whatever, is already presupposed, and we want to know where it comes from. Singer says of the property example that the maxim of the proposed action is that I am to steal whenever I wish to, and that this cannot be universalised because, if everyone were to steal whenever he wished to, property would cease to exist and so stealing would be impossible. Precisely. The original maxim, by describing the action as one of 'stealing', already presupposes the existence of property. That is Hegel's criticism. Similarly, it is futile for H.B. Acton to attempt to defend Kant by arguing that human society is inconceivable without property or, more plausibly, without promising.[6] To argue thus is to concede Hegel's point.

This point needs to be elaborated so as to reveal its full force. Hegel is suggesting, I think, that if such things as property or promising are presupposed, they carry with them certain *practical principles* which are also presupposed. If the existence of property is already given, then so is the principle that one ought not to steal, for this is built into the definition of property.[7] That, of course, is why there is a contradiction between stealing and the existence of property. Similarly, if the existence of promising is already given, then so is the principle that one ought not to break one's promises. But in that case Kant's categorical imperative, the requirement of universalisability, becomes redundant. It can simply be allowed to drop out altogether. For, at the point where it is applied, we are already in possession of universal practical principles, and so do not need the 'categorical imperative' in order to generate them.

This is where Hegel makes the transition to the concept of Sittlichkeit. In the examples we have been considering, what is significant is that the principles presupposed by universalisability are the principles of *social institutions*. And Hegel's claim (which he cannot, of course, base simply on these examples) is that practical principles in general derive from the institutions and practices of a human society. This is the source from which Kant's purely formal requirement gets its content. Kant is right in thinking that principles of action must have a universal character in order to be rational. But in that case they must be more than just universalisable; they must be actually universal, as the laws and customs which make up the spirit of a people.

7. This is a more radical claim than we have previously attributed to Hegel. Previously the claim was that social Sittlichkeit solves the traditional problem of ethics because men's basic need is for self-realization and this is possible only through the shared activities of a free nation. The stronger claim now is that principles of action.cannot even be *rational* unless they are rooted in social laws and customs. It is

difficult to pin Hegel down to any explicit assertion of this, but I think it can legitimately be ascribed to him, for his concept of Sittlichkeit is certainly offered as an alternative, not just to Kantian moral theory, but to all the previous six stages of the *Phenomenology*. And since they represent all the traditional attempts to provide a foundation for practical reasoning, it is fair to assume that Hegel's Sittlichkeit is intended to do the same.

The claim is a bold one and seems open to obvious objections.[8] It looks as if Hegel is begging the whole question of the status of social and political conformism. He appears to be implying that to rebel against the laws and customs of one's own society is not just undesirable, but irrational. And even the most ardent conservative is likely to regard this as rather a hasty move.

But the matter is not so simple. For if we interpret Hegel in this way, what are we to make of the fact that he sees Sittlichkeit personified in Antigone, the archetypal rebel against the state and political authority? In the play by Sophocles, Antigone's brothers Polyneices and Eteocles have fought one another for the crown of Thebes, and both have been killed in the battle. Creon, the new king, decrees that Polyneices, who has attacked the city, should for this reason be left unburied. He justifies his edict in terms of political necessity, but Antigone defies his order and gives her brother secret burial. She declares that human laws must be overriden by divine laws, laws which command the duties of a family to its dead and the duties of a sister to a brother. These laws are invoked when she says to Creon, in a speech from which Hegel quotes:

'I did not think your edicts strong enough
To overrule the unwritten unalterable laws
Of God and heaven, you being only a man.
They are not of yesterday or today, but everlasting,
Though where they came from, none of us can tell.'
(Sophocles *Antigone* 11.453-7 (Watling's translation p. 138).
Cf. *Phenomenology* p. 452).

It is clear, then, that if these are typical of what Hegel calls 'ethical laws', the latter are not to be identified simply with the laws promulgated by the political powers-that-be. The laws which Antigone obeys are still in an important sense *social* laws, the laws of a 'Volk'. They are the traditional rules of a community, handed down from generation to generation, the traditional means by which that community represents

81

to itself the meaning of death, of family ties, etc.

All this is confirmed in Hegel's subsequent description of 'The Ethical World'. The section is built entirely around the Antigone example. Sittlichkeit incorporates *both* human laws, exemplified in the laws of the state and the power of the government, *and* divine laws, associated particularly with the family and always in potential conflict with the laws of the state. There is in this section, and in the *Phenomenology* generally, none of that glorification of the state to which Hegel is inclined in the *Philosophy of Right* (and we must remember that, even in the latter work, Sittlichkeit still includes the family and civil society as well as the state). Moreover the family represents, for Hegel, the 'private' aspect of social life, the realm of individual interests and personal relationships. Hegel recognises (rightly) that the distinction between 'public' and 'private' falls *within* social life. Although there are certainly activities in which a man can be said to engage as a private individual, this does not mean that they involve him in complete isolation. They are still social, but they are concerned with his more immediate social relationships (love, friendship, familial relationships of parent and child, husband and wife, brother and sister, etc.); and according to Hegel they are still governed by social laws and customs.

Hegel's concept of Sittlichkeit, then, cannot be regarded as a sleight of hand intended to justify political conformism. But is it not a defence of social conformism in a more general sense – an adherence to the conventions and traditions of one's own society? Does it not require us to treat as irrational any radical criticism of conventional morality?

This charge is more difficult to rebut. Indeed, Hegel's position is not clear enough for us to be able to formulate a definite answer. Much depends on what he means by 'customs'. If they are defined simply as the ways in which most people usually behave within a particular society, then Hegel's position *would* be a sleight-of-hand conservativism. But Hegel is not as crude as this. He is never, as Marcuse would say, so 'one-dimensional'. His whole developmental logic must surely commit him to the recognition of contradictions within social life; of values implicit in people's behaviour which, if made explicit, would come into conflict with conventional assumptions. In the *Philosophy of Right,* Hegel remarks that 'even Plato's *Republic*, which passes proverbially as an empty ideal, is in essence nothing but an interpretation of the nature of Greek ethical life' (p. 10). This suggests that, for Hegel, the revolutionary and the reactionary appeal equally to 'customs' of their society, and that the conflict between them is a conflict between different tendencies within that society.

If we ask how a community can in fact embody ideals which are not realised, or only imperfectly realised, in current practice, an important part of the answer would be: in its art and literature, in its religious symbols, and in its philosophical thought. These are ways in which a society can represent to itself ideals which stand in judgment on its own present condition. Does Hegel include these among 'ethical customs'? Again, the answer is unclear. In the *Encyclopaedia,* art, religion and philosophy are higher stages than the ethical world – but 'higher than' does not, for Hegel, mean 'other than' (though we may be hard put to it to say what it does mean). In the *Phenomenology* they seem to be more closely related to the ethical realm; religion (in which art is included) is treated as the self-consciousness of a society. The very phrase 'the spirit of a people' seems to suggest something cultural or at any rate wider than explicit behavioural conventions.

We should remember also that Hegel distinguishes between 'immediate ethical substance' and 'conscious ethical substance'. He regards the critical attitude towards social conventions, which was introduced by the Sophists and by Socrates, as a progressive development of great historical importance, and looks to a synthesis of this with social ethics. The crucial question, then, is what form this synthesis is to take. Hegel never arrives at an answer in the *Phenomenology,* and the following passage in the *Philosophy of Right* displays all the unresolved ambiguities:

'Conscience is the expression of the absolute title of subjective self-consciousness to know in itself and from within itself what is right and obligatory, to give recognition only to what it thus knows as good, and at the same time to maintain that whatever in this way it knows and wills is in truth right and obligatory. Conscience as this unity of subjective knowing with what is absolute is a sanctuary which it would be sacrilege to violate. But . . . whether what conscience takes or declares to be good is actually so, is ascertainable only from the content of the good it seeks to realize. What is right and obligatory is the absolutely rational element in the will's volitions and therefore it is not in essence the *particular* property of an individual, and its form is not that of feeling or any other private (i.e. sensuous) type of knowing, but essentially that of universals determined by thought, i.e. the form of laws and principles. Conscience is therefore subject to the judgment of its truth or falsity . . . .

For this reason, the state cannot give recognition to conscience in its private form as subjective knowing. . .' (*Philosophy of Right* para. 137).

Does this mean that private judgments are rational only if they appeal to publicly-shared standards, or does it mean that the individual is rational only if he agrees with the *status quo*? The issue is unresolved.

Had Hegel been able to resolve it, he might have produced an acceptable ethical theory instead of just a suggestive one. At one point in the section on 'Reason as Testing Laws', Hegel says of ethical law that it is

'. . . not a *command* which merely *ought* to be, it *is*, and *has effect*.' (p. 451).

Hegel sees the 'is/ought' problem not, in the manner of contemporary philosophers, as the completely general problem of the relation between 'is' statements as a whole and 'ought' statements as a whole. For him, it is the problem of the relation between how men *ought to act* and how they *do act*.[9] And Hegel's basic conviction is that the former must *in some sense* be grounded in the latter. I would say that this is true. A contemporary attempt to defend such a position could draw on Wittgenstein's discussion of how rational judgments must appeal to public criteria, and of how these in turn are constituted by the shared judgments which people do actually make. Meanwhile the best defence of a specifically Hegelian ethical theory remains one which is provided not by Hegel but by Bradley, in the early part of 'My Station and its Duties':

'The child . . . is born . . . into a living world . . . . He does not even think of his separate self; he grows with his world, his mind fills and orders itself; and when he can separate himself from that world, and know himself apart from it, then by that time his self, the object of his self-consciousness, is penetrated, infected, characterized by the existence of others. Its content implies in every fibre relations of community. He learns, or already perhaps has learnt, to speak, and here he appropriates the common heritage of his race, the tongue that he makes his own is his country's language, it is . . . the same that others speak, and it carries into his mind the ideas and sentiments of the race . . . and stamps them in indelibly. He grows up in an atmosphere of example and general custom . . . . The soul within him is saturated, is filled, is qualified by, it has assimilated, has got its substance, has built itself up from, it *is* one and the same life with the universal life, and if he turns against this he turns against himself.' (Bradley: *Ethical Studies* pp. 171-2).

1   Bradley is particularly good on this — see *Ethical Studies*, pp. 163-174.

2   *Cf.* especially 'Private Property and Communism' in the *Economic and Philosophical Manuscripts of 1844.*

3   Hegel rather glosses over the fact of slavery in the Greek world. It is difficult to see how he can accommodate his view of the Greek city-state as an ethical community to the fact that it was a society founded on the master-slave relation. He takes more account of the fact in the *Philosophy of History* (e.g. p. 254f) but does not mention it in the 'Objective Spirit' section of the *Phenomenology*.

4   *Cf. Phenomenology* p.479. For a further discussion of Hegel's critique of ethical individualism in these sections, see A. MacIntyre: *A Short History of Ethics* pp. 206-9.

5   Marcus George Singer: *Generalization in Ethics* pp. 251 ff.

6   H.B. Acton: *Kant's Moral Philosophy* pp. 24-5.

7   This would be true regardless of whether the property in question were private property or communal property. I mention this because an interesting feature of Hegel's discussion in the *Phenomenology* is his comparison of private property and communal property. The discussion is confused and is of no great value in itself, but it is interesting that Hegel took the question seriously.

8   A convenient statement of such objections can be found in Ch. VIII of W.H. Walsh: *Hegelian Ethics.* Walsh thinks that Hegel can be defended to some extent, but in the end he allows that the objections carry considerable weight.

9   And so it is for Kant, whom Hegel can again be seen as criticising. *Cf. Critique of Pure Reason* A 319, B 375: 'Nothing is more reprehensible than to derive the laws prescribing what *ought to be done* from what *is done,* or to impose upon them the limits by which the latter is circumscribed.'

5

HISTORY AND ALIENATION

1. 'Spirit', the fourth of the six main divisions of the *Phenomenology,* is divided into three sections, corresponding to what Hegel regards as the three major historical epochs. For Hegel, the two turning-points of history are the breakdown and disappearance of the Greek city-states, and the French Revolution. Hence the three sections of 'Spirit' are:— A. 'Objective Spirit': the ethical world of the Greeks and its decline into the atomised society of the Roman Empire; B. 'Self-estranged Spirit': the period from the end of the ancient world to the French Revolution, i.e. the Christian, feudal world, and, at the end of this period, the rise of the bourgeoisie and its cultural expression in the Enlightenment, culminating in the Revolution; C. 'Spirit certain of itself': the post-Revolutionary world.

I have already said something about the first main section of 'Spirit', and I shall not add much here. The section is marred by Hegel's emphasis on the 'Antigone' example. He then has to use some rather desperate arguments in an attempt to show that the divine law *must* be epitomised in the duty to bury the dead, and that this duty *must* be specifically the duty of a sister to her brother.

But before moving on to the section on 'Self-estranged Spirit' it will be useful to look at Hegel's account of the disappearance of the Greek world. We have seen that he associates this with individualism — the individual no longer identifies himself immediately with society, and this development is represented by the ideas of the Sophists and Socrates. Hegel now adds a further dimension to this account. The seeds of individualism are already present within Greek society in the form of the family, as a social force potentially in conflict with the state. And whereas the man finds his fulfillment in the wider community, the woman finds hers within the family, in the pursuit of its limited interests. From the point of view of the state, therefore, woman is 'the enemy within the gates'. The spirit of individualism which she represents must be suppressed, and the principal means of suppressing it is war, for when the community is at war it becomes more cohesive and internal divisions recede into the background. In the long run, however, the expedient of warfare actually fosters the spirit of individualism, in two respects. In the first place it emphasises the individuality of the nation, as one community among others; and secondly, it brings to the fore the strong individual, the young man who possesses military prowess and physical strength. In this way the community sows the seeds of its own destruction. It prepares the way for a new, more individualistic form of social life to emerge, when 'the uniform solidarity . . . has burst into a plurality of separate points'. (p. 499).

This new form of society is to be found in the Roman Empire, which is discussed in the section on 'Legal Status'.

> 'The universal being thus split up into the atomic units of a sheer plurality of individuals, this inoperative lifeless spirit is a principle of equality in which all count for as much as each, i.e. have the significance of *Persons*.' (p. 501).

The claim to citizenship − 'Civis Romanus sum' − is not now a claim to active participation in the political life of the community, but merely a claim to certain legal rights, the rights of a 'person', a private citizen. And the content of social life now resides not in traditional laws and customs, which every member of the community could experience as the expression of his own activity, but in one who is, like everybody else, a single isolated individual − the emperor. His power is experienced by other individuals as completely alien, even though it is created only by their own submission to him and recognition of him. In order to maintain his power, the emperor must make it oppressive and destructive.

> 'The lord of the world becomes really conscious of what he is . . . by that power of destruction which he exercises against the contrasted selfhood of his subjects. For his power is not the spiritual union and concord in which the various persons might get to know their *own* self-consciousness. Rather they exist as persons separately for themselves . . . . They are, therefore, in a merely negative relation, a relation of exclusion both to one another and to him. . .'
> (p. 505).

The social world, then, is now experienced by individuals not as something in which they find confirmation of their own identity, but as something alien and hostile, although it is at the same time their own creation. This is the condition of alienation, and Hegel regards it as characterising European society throughout the succeeding centuries until the French Revolution.[1]

2. Here is Hegel's general description of alienation:

'That spirit whose self is absolutely insular, absolutely discrete, finds its content over against itself in the form of a reality that is just as impenetrable as itself, and the world here gets the characteristic of being something external, negative to self-consciousness. Yet this world is a spiritual reality, it is essentially the fusion of individuality with being. This its existence is the work of self-consciousness, but likewise an actuality immediately present and alien to it, which has a peculiar being of its own, and in which it does not know itself.' (p. 509).

This is alienation as a relation of the individual to the social world. It in turn gives rise to another level of alienation. Because alienated consciousness sees itself as cut off from objective reality, it projects its reunification with its object into another world, a 'beyond' which is a realm of pure consciousness. This remote other world is the world of religious faith, which Hegel therefore sees as an attempt to escape from the fragmentation of the real world. But just because this other world is a reflection of the real world, the reconciliation which it offers is itself presented in an alienated form, as the relation of man to God (cf. pp. 510-1 and 513). Alienation thus takes three forms: (i) alienation within the real world; (ii) alienation of the world of pure consciousness from the real world; (iii) alienation within the world of pure consciousness.

The distinction between the different levels of alienation determines the ensuing structure of 'Self-estranged Spirit'. Alienation in the real world is described in the section entitled 'Culture and its Realm of Reality'. Alienation in the world of pure consciousness is dealt with in the sections on 'Faith and Pure Insight'[2] and 'The Enlightenment'. Finally the return of the spirit of Enlightenment to the real world is signalled by the French Revolution, which Hegel discusses in 'Absolute Freedom and the Terror'.

The term translated as 'culture' in the title of the first section is 'Bildung'. This word could be variously translated as 'cultivation', 'education', 'development', etc. The emphasis here is on self-cultivation (which is probably the best translation, and is the one which I shall use). Hegel says:

'The means, then, whereby an individual gets validity and reality here is self-cultivation. The estrangement on the part of spirit from its natural existence is here the individual's true original nature and substance. The relinquishment of this natural state is therefore both his purpose and his mode of existence . . . . This individuality moulds itself by self-cultivation to what it is in itself, and only by so doing is it then something in itself and possesses real existence.' (p. 515).

The two means of self-cultivation which Hegel subsequently considers are political — the individual's subordination of himself to the power of the state — and economic — the production by the individual of wealth which has a universal value and is enjoyed by others besides himself. According to Hegel, then, the significance of these activities is, first, that the individual rises above his purely natural condition (there is something of an analogy here with Hobbes' account of how society is created by men's relinquishment of the state of nature). Secondly, Hegel considers that through this relinquishment of their natural condition, men create the social entities, state power and economic wealth, which are the objects of their activity. And thirdly, by this means men also create themselves, they give themselves objective reality. This 'self-cultivation' is therefore one with the notions of 'self-objectification' and 'self-realisation' which we have considered previously. However, within the self-estranged world, the world of atomic individuals, this objectification also takes on the form of *alienation*, as Hegel now proceeds to show.

State power and wealth are, then, the two aspects of spiritual substance in the self-estranged world. They are the objectification of the two aspects of consciousness, being-in-itself and being-for-itself. State power corresponds to being-in-itself; it represents the universal aspect of consciousness, the denial of independent individuality. It is

'the simple spiritual substance, . . . wherein individuals find their essential nature expressed, and where their particular existence is simply and solely a consciousness of their own universality.' (p. 520).

Wealth represents the aspect of being-for-itself, of independent individual activity, since in his economic activity each individual sees himself as acting for himself and in his own interests. Nevertheless wealth too is implicitly universal — 'it becomes manifest that in his own enjoyment

89

each gives enjoyment to all, in his own labour each works for all as well as for himself, and all for him'. (p. 520).

Towards these two objective entities, consciousness can stand in a relation of either harmony or discord. The consciousness which is in harmony with them Hegel defines as 'the noble consciousness'. It willingly acquiesces in the authority of the state and renders obedient service; it receives wealth from others, acknowledges its gratitude and considers itself indebted to the provider of wealth. The opposite attitude is taken by what Hegel calls 'the base consciousness'.

'It looks upon the authoritative power of the state as a chain, as something suppressing its being-for-itself, and hence hates the ruler, obeys only with secret malice, and stands ever ready to burst out in rebellion.' (p. 525).

Similarly it regards the enjoyment of wealth as something merely evanescent, as confirmation of its own isolated existence.

With the descriptions of the noble and the base consciousness, we arrive at a definite historical reference. Nowhere in the *Phenomenology* are there precise references to historical events. Historical epochs are described in general terms, and are not identified explicitly. Hegel never says, in so many words, that the ethical world is that of the Greek city-states, or that the self-estranged world is that of feudalism. (This is deliberate, and symptomatic of Hegel's view of history, as we shall see). Nevertheless the account of the noble and the base consciousness must refer to the division in feudal society between the nobility and the common people. In the dialectical section of 'Culture and its Realm of Reality', the roles of the noble and base consciousness come to be reversed. The noble consciousness becomes aware of its real alienation from the state and from wealth, it recognises that beneath the apparent harmony its real attitude is one of rebellion and resentment. The base consciousness for its part becomes aware of its real power, and comes to recognise both the state and wealth as realms in which it can affirm itself. In this we must see, formulated in very general terms, Hegel's account of the decline of feudalism and the rise of the bourgeoisie.

The change in the attitude of the noble consciousness towards state power comes about as follows. At first the noble is in harmony with the power of the state. His attitude is

'the heroism of service; the virtue which sacrifices individual being to the universal, and thereby brings this into existence; the type of personality which of itself renounces possession and enjoyment, acts for the sake of the prevailing power, and in this way becomes a concrete reality.' (p. 527).

However, this attitude of heroic service cannot be sustained in its extreme form. This would require the noble to sacrifice not just his interests but his own life for the sake of his feudal superior. But to do this would be to frustrate the very function of such service, which is that the noble should find a confirmation of his own identity in the object to which he sacrifices himself. What he requires, therefore, is a form of sacrifice in which he 'gives himself up as completely as in the case of death, but at the same time preserves himself in the renunciation' (p. 529). And this, Hegel suggests, is to be found in a form of self-renunciation which takes place not in *action* but only in *language,* in mere words.

On this dubious basis Hegel posits a transition from the 'heroism of service' to the 'heroism of flattery', an ironic label for the activity of the courtier who takes the place of the feudal lord. Since the noble's self-abasement is now actualised only in words, and therefore costs nothing, it can be absolute. Consequently the king can be treated to the most extravagant and sycophantic flattery from the nobility, who are 'grouped as an ornamental setting round the throne, and are for ever telling him, who sits on the throne, what he is' (p. 534). The king is thereby raised to a pinnacle of authority, to the status of an absolute monarch.

However, since this exalted status is created and sustained entirely by the homage of the nobles, the real power of the state has effectively passed to them. The absolute power of the monarch consists simply in the name by which he is addressed — it is based solely on words. And the real attitude of the noble consciousness has now become explicit. Originally it adopted a stance of harmony with the power of the state, but its true nature turns out to consist rather in retaining its independence even when it is supposedly rendering service. Its real relation to the state is not harmony but discord. It now becomes openly apparent that the noble consciousness is no longer distinct from the base consciousness. The latter 'has gained its end, that of subordinating universal power to self-centred isolation of self' (p. 536).

The dialectical process, then, has been that of making explicit the real alienation of the noble consciousness from the state. Hegel apparently sees this alienation as having been always implicit in the noble consciousness. In this world there is an inevitable gulf between the state and the individual. The state is no longer, like the Greek city-state, the embodiment of the spirit of a people. It is no longer the source of the individual's cultural and ethical life. The 'state', so-called, is simply the king or the emperor, the peak of the feudal hierarchy but, for all that, simply another individual. This is why other individuals cannot recognise themselves in the state, why it must be, for them, something alien. Hegel's view seems to be, therefore, that the base consciousness, with its attitude of rebelliousness, is the true consciousness of the relation between the state and the individual, a relation which is concealed by the attitude of service on the part of the noble consciousness.

The attitude of the noble consciousness towards wealth undergoes a similar change. Wealth is the expression of being-for-itself; the noble consciousness ought therefore to find in it that confirmation of its independent individuality which it failed to find in state power. But it cannot do so. Its relation to wealth is that of the *consumer*; it receives wealth from the hands of another. Consequently, instead of finding there a confirmation of its independence, it finds rather its dependence on another individual, the producer.

> 'It finds itself face to face with its own self as such in a state of estrangement, as an objective solid actuality which it has to take from the hands of another being-for-itself . . . . It sees its self under the power of an alien will on which it depends for the concession of itself.' (p. 537)

Thus the noble's relation to wealth, also, changes from harmony to discord. His gratitude towards the provider of wealth is replaced by resentment.

The dialectic of wealth is also described by Hegel from the point of view of the base consciousness (pp. 538^{32}-540^2). The base consciousness is the producer of wealth. Previously it had experienced wealth merely as a transitory enjoyment. It now becomes aware of the power which it wields through its production of wealth, 'knowing . . . that what it dispenses becomes the self of someone else'. It thus acquires a new confidence, a new concord with its object, and 'in place of revolt appears arrogance' (p. 539).

The reversal of roles is completed. The noble consciousness and the base consciousness have changed places. And this reflects a more general change.

'What is found out in this sphere is that neither the concrete realities, state-power and wealth, nor their determinate conceptions, good and bad, nor the consciousness of good and bad (the consciousness that is noble and the consciousness that is base) possess real truth; it is found that all these moments are inverted and transmuted the one into the other, and each is the opposite of itself.' (p. 541).

This process of transmutation is, of course, a particular guise for the dialectic. In this particular context, Hegel finds it expressed in the language of witty paradoxes which he illustrates from Diderot's dialogue *Le neveu de Rameau*. The character Rameau, in his ironic presentation of the duplicities and deceptions of his society, employs a language which Hegel sees as exactly expressing the principle that everything turns into its opposite. Rameau is the type of what Hegel calls the 'disintegrated consciousness'; just because he participates unashamedly in the vanities and deceptions of his society, he sees through them and recognises them for what they are. Reified social institutions become transparent to him, and he therefore prefigures, for Hegel, the overcoming of alienation.

'State-power and wealth are the real and actually acknowledged forms of power. But . . . just by the fact that it gets the mastery over them it knows them to be not real by themselves, know rather itself to be the power within them, and them to be vain and empty.' (p. 547).

3. The dialectic of wealth repeats the essential features of the dialectic of master and slave. The noble consciousness, like the master, fails to objectify itself through wealth because it is related to wealth solely as consumer, whereas the base consciousness, like the slave, is the producer for whom wealth is the expression of his own power. The dialectic of wealth is also the aspect of alienation which is closest to the account given by Marx, for whom the fundamental form of alienation is alienated labour. In this case, however, important differences begin to emerge. Hegel, for example, has said that the base consciousness becomes aware of wealth as the expression of its own power when it recognises that it produces for others to consume and that it thereby places others in a position of dependence. Thus Hegel sees the producer as escaping from alienation to that extent, whereas Marx sees the worker as alienated just because he works for another. But of course the phrase 'works for another' is much too general. The worker under capitalism 'works for

another' not simply in the general sense that he produces what others consume, but in the sense that he does not own or control the means of production, and that consequently his work is imposed on him, it is significant for him solely as the means to a wage, the product of his labour belongs to the capitalist, etc. Hegel does not make these distinctions. His notion of the 'base consciousness' as producer of wealth incorporates equally the factory-owner, the craftsman, the wage-labourer, or whatever. Even the category of 'producer' which I have attributed to Hegel is more specific than his own terminology. He talks simply of 'the spirit of wealth', or even just of 'wealth' (it is to 'wealth', for example, that he attributes 'arrogance' − p. 539). He fails to take any real account of the concrete nature of specific economic relations.

I shall try to show the wider significance of this difference between Hegel and Marx by considering Marx's own criticisms of Hegel. I want to approach the problem by looking briefly at the sections which follow 'Culture and its Realm of Reality'. My intention is not to give a general account of them, but to look specifically at Hegel's view of the relation between alienation in the real world and alienation in the realm of pure consciousness.

4. Let us first recall the terms in which Hegel has previously described the relation.

'The sphere of spirit at this stage breaks up into two regions. The one is the actual world, that of self-estrangment, the other is that which spirit constructs for itself in the ether of pure consciousness, raising itself above the first. This second world, being constructed in opposition and contrast to that estrangement, is just on that account not free from it; on the contrary, it is only the other form of that very estrangement . . . . It is faith, in so far as faith is a flight from the actual world.' (p. 513).

There are two important points to be emphasised here. First, there is the clear implication that the world of religious faith is an *illusory* world. It is an attempt to escape from the real world, but a futile attempt, since the world of pure consciousness is, in itself, empty, it has no content. Hence the second point: since religious faith cannot derive its content from pure consciousness, it must derive it from the real world. The content of religious belief is an idealised reflection of the content of the real world. It is a 'reflection out of the world of culture' (p. 551), it is 'nothing else than the real world lifted into the universality of pure consciousness' (p. 554). More specifically, Hegel attempts to show, in the section on 'Faith and Pure Insight', that the relations between being-in-itself and being-for-itself, state-power and wealth in the realm of culture find their idealised expression in the doctrine of the Trinity and the relation between God the Father and God the Son.

Religious faith yields to the rationalistic criticism of the Enlightenment. But Enlightenment philosophy is likewise an attitude of pure consciousness, and is equally incapable of generating its own content from within itself. Its doctrines derive, in fact, from the alienated experience inherited from religion. It perpetuates the split between Absolute Being and the isolated individual consciousness. The former is reduced to an empty abstraction – the God of Deism, or the materialist concept of 'substance'. The positive emphasis is now on the other side of the relation – on the immediacy of the individualistic consciousness, expressed in the epistemology of sensationalism and the ethic of utilitarianism.

Concerning these sections of the *Phenomenology*, then, the general point to be made is this. Religious faith and Enlightenment rationalism are alike set apart from the real world in a realm of pure consciousness. As such, they are devoid of content. Their content is therefore a reflection of the alienated experience of the real world. Alienation in thought is, for Hegel, a reflection of social alienation.

This point can be extended. I would say that it applies not just to these particular sections of the *Phenomenology,* but is a central principle of the work as a whole. Notice first that many of the forms of thought examined elsewhere in the *Phenomenology* are explicitly assigned a historical location within the alienated world. 'Sense-certainty' is seen to be identified with the sensationalism of the Enlightenment (p. 577). Within the section of 'Self-consciousness', Stoicism and Scepticism are to be located in the world of Legal Status where alienation first makes its appearance; Hegel says there:

'What in Stoicism was implicit merely in an abstract way, is now an explicit concrete world. Stoicism is nothing else than the mood of consciousness which reduces to its abstract form the principle of legal status, the principle of the sphere of right.' (p. 502).

And a little later he states:

'Formerly we saw the stoical independence of pure thought pass through Scepticism and find its truth in the "unhappy consciousness"

95

. . . . If this knowledge appeared at that stage merely as the one-sided view of a consciousness *qua* consciousness, here the actual truth of that view has made its appearance. The truth consists in the fact that this universal accepted objectivity of self-consciousness is reality estranged from it.' (p. 506).

In other words, the Unhappy Consciousness is a form of pure conscious-ness whose underlying reality is the world of self-estrangement. (Hence, of course, the close relation between the section on the Unhappy Consciousness and Hegel's account of Faith).

Again, Hegel's description of Pure Insight makes it clear that he identifies it with the forms of thought discussed in the various sections of 'Reason':

'Its aim thus is to cancel every kind of independence which falls without self-consciousness, whether that be the independence of the actually objective or of the inherently real, and to mould it into conceptual form. It not merely is the certainty of self-conscious reason assured of being all truth; it knows that it is so.' (p. 557).

And we have seen that the stages of practical Reason, in particular, are (in the introduction to 'Self-realization of Rational Self-consciousness') assigned by Hegel to the self-estranged world.

So much by way of enumeration. But we can also explain in general terms why the fact of social alienation should be basic to all the forms of thought discussed in the *Phenomenology*. The declared aim of the *Phenomenology* is to reconcile subject and object — that is, the subject *of knowledge* and the object of knowledge. All the forms of thought which are examined — prior to Absolute Knowledge — are characterised by a split between subject and object. Each stage is one-sided. It affirms the subject at the expense of the object, or vice versa; it affirms the individual at the expense of the universal, or vice versa. I suggest that Hegel sees these divisions within consciousness as the product of the divisions within the social world, isolating the individual from others and thus alienating him from the social object. In that case, *all* the forms of thought in the first half of the *Phenomenology* stand in the same relation to the alienated world as do Faith and Enlightenment — they are 'nothing else than the real world lifted into the universality of pure consciousness', they are *reflections* of the alienated world and are 'just on that account not free from it.' And this hypothesis makes good sense of the structure of the *Phenomenology*. Its starting point, in

Sense-certainty, is the completely alienated consciousness, the isolated individual spectator. In the course of the first half it is shown that self-consciousness presupposes *agency* and *work*; thus consciousness cannot now be viewed as completely cut off from its real object, it is immersed in the real world and works upon it. It also emerges that self-consciousness presupposes relations with other self-consciousnesses and, eventually, that it presupposes a world of co-operative work, mutual recognition and universal freedom — an unalienated social world. But it is not enough for such a world to be presupposed in thought, it must be brought about historically, and Hegel therefore has to embark upon a survey of the necessary historical development, for only with the overcoming of social alienation can the alienation of consciousness also be overcome. In the light of this interpretation, it is not too much to say that the account of the Self-estranged World is the heart of the *Phenomenology*.

5. What is the relevance of all this to Marx's criticism of Hegel? Consider the following quotations from Marx's 'Critique of Hegel's Dialectic and General Philosophy':

> 'For Hegel, . . . the alienation of self-consciousness is not regarded as the *expression,* reflected in knowledge and thought, of the *real* alienation of human life. Instead, *actual* alienation, that which appears real, is in its *innermost* hidden nature (which philosophy first discloses) only the *phenomenal being* of the alienation of real human life, of *self-consciousness.*' (Karl Marx: *Early Writings,* p. 204).

Or again:

> 'The appropriation of man's objectified and alienated faculties is thus, in the first place, only an appropriation which occurs in *consciousness,* in *pure thought,* i.e. in *abstraction.* It is the appropriation of these objects as *thoughts* and as *movements of thought.* For this reason, . . . there is already implicit in the *Phenomenology* . . . the uncritical idealism of Hegel's later works.' (*Ibid.,* p. 201).

Now, in a way, this criticism is unjust. I have been trying to show that Hegel does present the alienation of self-consciousness precisely as 'the *expression,* reflected in knowledge and thought, of the *real* alienation of human life'. Even the Marxist concept of 'ideology' would not be out of place in the *Phenomenology* to describe the status of the forms of thought there. For the same reason it seems unjust to say that Hegel

97

looks to the overcoming of alienation within pure thought. I have suggested on the contrary that Hegel sees the overcoming of alienation in thought as requiring the return of pure thought to the real world, and therefore as depending on the overcoming of social alienation.

We should, then, be on guard against too easy a criticism of Hegel. It is one of Hegel's most important achievements, and an advance on all previous philosophy, that he does locate forms of consciousness, including philosophical theories, in a social and historical context, and does identify significant connections between the one and the other. Nevertheless, at a deeper level Marx's criticisms are valid. The trouble with Hegel's account is that, having brought the alienation of pure thought back to its roots in social alienation, *he then treats social alienation as itself an alienation of consciousness.* Consider again his statement of how alienation comes about:

> '. . . the individual, as he immediately finds his existence in the actual objective social order, in the life of his nation, has a solid imperturbable *confidence*; the universal mind has not for him resolved itself into abstract moments, and thus, too, he *does not think* of himself as existing in singleness and independence. When however he has once arrived at this *knowledge,* as indeed he must, this immediate unity with mind, this undifferentiated existence in the substance of mind, his naive confidence, is lost. Isolated by himself he is himself now the central essential reality − no longer universal mind.' (p. 379 − my italics).

The emergence of alienation is here presented as a change in consciousness − not, indeed, a change within 'pure thought', but a change in the attitude of consciousness towards the social world. The individual comes to *think* of the social object in a different way, he becomes *aware* of his independence from the social substance. Here is the real difference between Hegel and Marx. For Marx, alienation comes about as a change in the actual relations of production; if the individual comes to see the social product as something foreign to him, this is because it *is* foreign, it belongs to another.

> 'If the product of labour does not belong to the worker, but confronts him as an alien power, this can only be because it belongs to *a man other than the worker.*' (Karl Marx: *Early Writings* p. 130).

Again, if we look at Hegel's description of the world of Culture, we have to agree with Marx that

'When Hegel conceives wealth, the power of the state, etc. as entities alienated from the human being, he conceives them only in their thought form.' (Ibid., p. 200).

Most obviously, there is the fact that Hegel is concerned with the relations of state-power and wealth to the noble *consciousness* and the base *consciousness*. And this is not just an unfortunate piece of terminology, it is genuinely indicative of Hegel's approach. When for example, he describes the relations of 'harmony' and 'discord', he asserts that the noble, when it 'regards' state power, '*sees* that it has there its own nature pure and simple and the sphere for the exercise of its own powers'; similarly 'in the sphere of wealth, it *sees* that wealth secures for it the consciousness of being-for-itself', and 'hence it *looks upon* wealth likewise as something essential in relation to itself' (p. 525). The base consciousness '*looks upon* the authoritative power of the state as a chain', and it '*sees*, too, in wealth. . . merely something discordant'. It subsequently cancels its attitude of discordance when it becomes 'a power *aware* that it is independent and voluntary, and *knowing* at the same time that what it dispenses becomes the self of someone else' (p. 539).

These passages show, indeed, that alienation is not, for Hegel, constituted by the most *explicit* and *superficial* attitudes of consciousness. When he asserts that the noble consciousness initially adopts an attitude of harmony towards state-power and wealth, he nevertheless implies that it is, in reality, alienated from these objects. But when Hegel implies this, what he means is that the *underlying attitude* of the noble consciousness is one of secret rebellion. Alienation is constituted by the most deep-seated *attitudes* of consciousness towards its object. Whether or not consciousness is alienated depends exclusively on what it *thinks*.

In the first half of the *Phenomenology*, Hegel's preoccupation with consciousness is perfectly legitimate. His concerns there are, first and foremost, epistemological. Accordingly, in this context, alienation consists in the reification of objects which are really, in an important sense, constituted by human thought and therefore amenable to human understanding. The objects of sense-certainty, for example, are treated as simply given, whereas in fact they exist as objects for knowledge only because consciousness works on them and brings them under concepts. In such a case, then, the overcoming of alienation rightly takes the form of a change in the way of regarding the object. It is, as Marx says, a re-appropriation of the object for thought, a confirmation of it as a moment of thought. But though Marx's description is correct, I do not think that at this point it constitutes a sufficient ground for criticism of Hegel.

It becomes a valid criticism, however, when we turn to the second half of the *Phenomenology*. Hegel's mistake is to treat the second half as a continuation of the first. He describes a historical development as though it were simply a process of increasing knowledge. The overcoming of alienation in the social world is thus seen as the *recognition* by *consciousness* that its objects are its own creation.

This has two important consequences:

(a) As Marx says, it blunts the critical edge of Hegel's analyses. The accounts of state-power and wealth provide the basis for a radical criticism of political and economic alienation, but what Hegel actually supplies is 'a concealed, unclear and mystifying criticism' (Marx p. 202), and for the following reason. Hegel has revealed that the state is constituted by the alienation of human powers; it is created by the actions of individuals, but then confronts them as a hostile power over which they have no control. Therefore the overcoming of this alienation ought to mean, and for Marx it would mean, the *abolition of the state* as an independent entity, and the bringing of political life under cooperative human control. Similarly the overcoming of the alienation of wealth ought to mean the *abolition of private property,* and the exercise of cooperative control over economic life. For Hegel, however, alienation is overcome simply in the *recognition* that State-power and wealth are human creations. Previously, in the case of sense-certainty, the disappearance of alienation did not of course require the abolition of the objects of sense-certainty; rather, it involved the confirmation of them as objects of human experience. So now, Hegel treats state-power and wealth in the same way. When consciousness recognises that these are its own creation, it is, according to Hegel, no longer alienated from them but finds itself at home in them. Marx comments:

> 'Thus reason is at home in unreason as such. Man, who has recognised that he leads an alienated life in law, politics, etc., leads his true human life in this alienated life as such.' (*Op.cit.*, p. 210).

The case of religion is slightly different, insofar as this *is* genuinely an alienation within thought and is rightly treated by Hegel as such. But essentially the same point can still be made. Hegel has characterised religious faith as a form of alienation. He has described the world of Faith as a world 'which spirit constructs for itself in the ether of pure consciousness, raising itself above [the real world]' (p. 513). So, again, the overcoming of this alienation ought to consist in the abolition of religion. For Hegel, on the contrary, it means the recognition of religion as a human product and therefore as an authentic aspect of human experience.

'. . . self-conscious man, in so far as he has recognized and super-seded the spiritual world, . . . then confirms it again in this alienated form and presents it as his true existence; he re-establishes it and claims to *be at home in his other being*. Thus, for example, after superseding religion, when he has recognized religion as a product of self-alienation, he then finds a confirmation of himself in religion as religion.' (Marx, *op.cit.*, p. 210).

Marx's general conclusion seems irresistible:

'There can no longer be any question about Hegel's compromise with religion, the state, etc., for this falsehood is the falsehood of his whole argument.' (*Op.cit.*, p. 210).

(b) The second important consequence of Hegel's confused view of the relation between history and epistemology is that it distorts the real nature of historical change. Hegel writes as though the breakdown of the ancient world, and the emergence of the self-estranged world, were due simply to a change in consciousness. That, of course, is nonsense. It is also dangerous nonsense insofar as it suggests that the self-estranged world can be made to disappear in the same way. Marx sees it as leading directly to the illusions of the Left Hegelians. It also represents the illu-sions of political utopians in general, whose response to existing social evils is to call for a revolutionary change – in attitudes.
6. Both these consequences of Hegel's confusion are well illustrated in his account of the French Revolution. This occupies the final section of 'Self-estranged Spirit' and is entitled 'Absolute Freedom and the Terror'. Consciousness, as a result of its experience of Culture, of Faith, and of the Enlightenment, has come to recognise the emptiness alike of social entities such as the State and Wealth, and of the Absolute Being proclaimed by religion and philosophy. It has found that the rea-lity of all substantial entities consists in their relation to consciousness itself. This attitude is exemplified in the philosophy of Utilitarianism, which views everything in terms of its usefulness for the self. Translated into action, it

'. . . Brings on the scene spirit in the form of absolute freedom. It is the mode of self-consciousness which clearly comprehends that in its certainty of self lies the essence of all the component spiritual spheres of the real world and of the supersensible world . . . . The world is for it absolutely its own will, and this will is universal will.' (p. 600).

This 'general will' (the alternative translation emphasises the reference to Rousseau) therefore proceeds to abolish all traditional social institutions, all social ranks and classes. Treating them as a threat to its own autonomy, it 'puts itself on the throne of the world'.

In this activity of the general will, however, Hegel sees foreshadowed the Revolution's own self-destruction. The general will can accomplish nothing positive. It can create no effective social institutions of its own. Each government, each ruling group, becomes a faction in relation to the general will, and as such invites its own destruction. 'The only work and deed of universal freedom is therefore *death*' (p. 605); inexorably, the general will manifests itself as the Terror. Nothing positive and substantial can be accomplished until specific social roles are re-established, and individuals see themselves not simply as members of an amorphous 'general will' but as occupying their own particular sphere of social life.

'These individuals, who felt the fear of death, their absolute lord and master, submit to negation and distinction once more, arrange themselves under the "spheres", and return to a restricted and apportioned task, but thereby to their substantial reality.' (p. 607).

(Presumably the reference here is to the social order instituted by Napoleon, putting an end to the first phase of the Revolution).

A problem is hereby posed. It seems that the Revolution must lead inevitably to the restoration of an established social order, with its social ranks and classes. The prospect of any real progress therefore seems to vanish, along with any possibility of overcoming alienation in the social world. In its place there opens up the prospect of a recurrent cycle: men are confronted by alien social powers, they overthrow these and assert their own freedom, and then return once more to an alienated social order — 'Spirit would have anew to traverse and continually repeat this cycle of necessity' (p. 607).

But Hegel does not accept this prospect. For although, in social terms, there has been a return to the previous state of affairs, there has nevertheless been a *change in consciousness.* Through the experience of the Terror, consciousness has seen the objective social world disappear into sheer nothingness. In the self-estranged world of Culture, the alien reality set over against consciousness had a filling and a content; for the noble consciousness, it was the world of honour, for the base consciousness it was the world of wealth, for the believing consciousness it was a religious content, and so on. But

> '. . . all these determinations disappear with the disaster and ruin that overtakes the self in the state of absolute freedom.' (p. 608).

Even the general will, the sole spiritual substance of the world of absolute freedom, has turned out to be sheer nothingness. And so, having experienced the fact that none of these entities has an independent existence apart from the individual self, consciousness 'knows itself to be essential reality' (p. 609).

The implication is, then, that though consciousness now returns to a world of specified social roles and institutions, it no longer experiences these as alien, since it knows them to be the expression of its own self. Hegel had said:

> 'Spirit would have anew to traverse and continually repeat this cycle of necessity, *if* only complete interpenetration of self-consciousness and the substance were the result: an interpenetration in which self-consciousness, which has experienced the force of its universal nature operating negatively upon it, would try to know and find itself not as this particular self-consciousness but only as universal, and hence too would be able to endure the objective reality of universal spirit, a reality excluding self-consciousness as a particular.' (p. 607, my italics).

But, Hegel implies, this is *not* what has happened. The individual self-consciousness is *not* simply re-absorbed into the universal spirit. It now knows that this universal spirit is the expression of its own individual self.

At this point the Marxist criticism is apposite. For Hegel, alienation is overcome purely *within consciousness,* simply by the *recognition* that the social substance is not something alien. As Hegel himself says, the *Phenomenology* here takes flight from the social world into the world of thought —

> '. . . absolute freedom leaves its self-destructive sphere of reality, and passes over into another land of self-conscious Spirit, where in this

unreality freedom is taken to be and is accepted as the truth.' (p. 610).

[1] The terms 'alienation' and 'estrangement', both of which are employed in Baillie's translation, are interchangeable. They are both translations of 'Entfremdung'.

[2] Both the term 'insight' and Baillie's translation of 'Glaube' as 'belief' are liable to be misleading. Hegel's concern is with the opposition between faith and reason.

6

ABSOLUTE KNOWLEDGE

1. The French Revolution, then, is seen by Hegel as the overcoming of alienation; and alienation is overcome with the emergence of a new form of consciousness, one which is aware of its own 'absolute freedom', and is aware of 'the world absolutely in the form of consciousness'. What now remains is for this new consciousness to be given adequate expression, and this is the task of the rest of the *Phenomenology*. Hegel had already indicated the need for this at the beginning of the Preface. There, too, speaking of the change brought about by the French Revolution, he had said:

'. . . our epoch is a birth-time, and a period of transition. The spirit of man has broken with the old order of things hitherto prevailing, and with the old ways of thinking, and is in the mind to let them all sink into the depths of the past and to set about its own transformation. . . . The spirit of the time, growing slowly and quietly ripe for the new form it is to assume, disintegrates one fragment after another of the structure of its previous world. . . . This gradual crumbling to pieces, which did not alter the general look and aspect of the whole, is interrupted by the sunrise, which, in a flash and at a single stroke, brings to view the form and structure of the new world. But this new world is perfectly realized just as little as the new-born child . . . . It comes on the stage to begin with in its immediacy, in its bare generality. A building is not finished when its foundation is laid; and just as little is the attainment of a general concept of a whole the whole itself . . . . Science, the crowning glory of a spiritual world, is not found complete in its initial stages.' (pp. 75-6).

So, at the stage we have reached in the *Phenomenology* the new consciousness has emerged, but it has still to be fully developed and expressed.

Hegel first looks for this adequate expression in German philosophy, the philosophy of his immediate predecessors, and this he does in the last of the three sections of 'Spirit', entitled 'Spirit certain of itself: Morality'. He examines Kant's moral philosophy again, this time focusing on Kant's talk of moral *autonomy* and seeing this as a philosophical analogue of 'absolute freedom'. But he finds in Kant a pervasive ambivalence. Kant oscillates between seeing the moral consciousness as that of the autonomous moral agent, and seeing it as a reified consciousness having its object 'away outside itself, as something beyond itself' (p. 629). This is apparent in the so-called 'postulates of practical reason'. Kant now sets moral action in absolute antithesis to personal fulfilment, now postulates an ultimate harmony between the two. Similarly he sees morality and the natural inclinations now as being in inevitable conflict, now as being ultimately in harmony. In short, Kant's moral world-view still retains the divisions and antagonisms of an alienated consciousness. And Hegel finds equally unsatisfactory the moral philosophy of Fichte and the ideas of the German romantics ('the Beautiful Soul'), involving as they do a retreat into an inner subjectivity.

Hegel now turns to the examination of Religion (the subject-matter of the fifth of the six basic divisions of the *Phenomenology*). He looks there for an adequate social consciousness, because he sees this as the essential function of religion; in its religion a society expresses its own consciousness of itself. Hegel deals first with Eastern religions, then with ancient Greek religion (which he sees as 'the religion of art' and so is enabled to incorporate a discussion of aesthetics into the *Phenomenology*), and finally with Christianity, which he terms 'Revealed Religion'. I shall not examine here his treatment of any of the three. I have previously (in looking at the Unhappy Consciousness) referred to Hegel's view of religion in general and of Christianity in particular, and essentially the same view is repeated here, though with more emphasis on the positive aspect. As before, the most important feature of Christianity is seen to be the doctrine of the Incarnation, representing the truth that 'the divine nature is the same as the human' (p. 760), that absolute being is identical with self-consciousness. But although Christianity thereby expresses the overcoming of alienation, the unity of self and object, it does so in what is still an alienated form. It expresses conceptual truths in the form of pictorial images. The unity of self and object becomes the unity of man and God in the person of Christ; but because this unity is represented by a particular individual, it remains something alien to self-consciousness. The content of the religious consciousness is a 'true content' but lacks its 'true form', and so

consciousness 'must necessarily pass to a higher plane of mental development, where the absolute substance is not intuitively apprehended but
conceptually comprehended' (p. 764). This 'higher plane' is Absolute
Knowledge, the culmination of the *Phenomenology*, where religion gives
way to philosophy.

2. The truth grasped by Absolute Knowledge is, then, an awareness of
the reconciliation of subject and object. Consciousness knows its object
to be nothing other than itself (pp. 789-790). Already in the Introduction it had been indicated that this unification of subject and object,
in some sense, would be the goal of the *Phenomenology*. What we can
now reasonably ask is that here, at the point where Hegel claims that
Absolute Knowledge has been reached, he should be able to furnish
some account of what is *meant* by 'the reconciliation of subject and
object'.

He asserts, in fact, that this meaning is to be elucidated by recalling
the various stages through which consciousness has passed. This is an
important assertion. Hegel does *not* regard Absolute Knowledge as some
new and qualitatively different mode of cognition which consciousness
is to reach by leaving behind all its previous forms of experience. On
the contrary, Absolute Knowledge is nothing but the totality of those
previous forms. In this respect Hegel's position is to be clearly distinguished from that of such 'Hegelians' as F. H. Bradley.

Hegel proceeds to specify three previous forms of consciousness
which 'determine the ways in which consciousness must know the
object as itself' (p. 790). These are 'Reason as Observation', and in
particular the section on 'Physiognomy and Phrenology'; the doctrine
of utility in 'The Enlightenment'; and the Kantian 'Moral View of the
World'. It is surprising that Hegel should have picked out these particular stages of the *Phenomenology* to illustrate the various aspects of
the 'reconciliation of subject and object'. They serve the purpose, but
it cannot be said that they make his meaning very clear. There are
many other sections to which he could have referred. Indeed, he could
profitably have recalled the substance of each of the main divisions of
the *Phenomenology*; and if we do that now, it may throw rather more
light on Hegel's meaning.

Consciousness: The dominant theme here amounted to a denial that
the object of experience is simply 'given'. It can be experienced only
insofar as it is 'conceptualised', worked on by being brought under concepts. The conclusion of the section was therefore that, in this sense,
the object of consciousness is itself the product of consciousness.

Consciousness knows what it has itself put there, and to that extent, in knowing its object, it knows itself. In particular, there is no unknowable 'thing-in-itself' beyond the reach of consciousness.

Self-consciousness: Here the emphasis was on work in the *practical* sphere, and on the necessity of work for self-knowledge. The subject knows itself by objectifying itself. In 'The Unhappy Consciousness' Hegel looked at the ways in which consciousness fails to recognise its self-objectification as its own self. Its learning to do so is hailed, at the end of the section, as the dawn of Reason. Consciousness thereby comes to enjoy a confidence in the power and scope of reason, and an assurance that the world itself is rational.

Reason: What emerges from this section is the *social* character of human thought and action, of theoretical concepts and of practical norms. Thus the reconciliation of subject and object here takes the form of the reconciliation of the individual with society.

Spirit: The history of Spirit leads up to the reconciliation of social subject with social object, the 'social object' being the objects of political and economic action — state-power and wealth. Spirit comes to recognise that these are its own product. They therefore cease to exist as alien and independent objects, and correspondingly, in the theoretical realm, so do the 'absolute being' of faith and the 'absolute being' of enlightenment philosophy.

Religion: Within the sphere of religion, subject and object are reconciled in Christianity, in the doctrine of the unity of God and man. Insofar as this unity is represented in pictorial terms, it still preserves a division between subject and object, which is to be overcome in a form of consciousness higher than that of religion.

This recapitulation of the main stages of the *Phenomenology* permits us to make some further remarks about what Hegel means by 'the reconciliation of subject and object'.

(i) The phrase connotes what we have also been referring to as *the overcoming of alienation*. It should by now be obvious that the two are different sides of the same coin.

(ii) The phrase is closely linked with Hegel's emphasis on *work*. The theme of work, understood both as theoretical work and as practical work, is central to the *Phenomenology*. It is through work that man can achieve self-knowledge (man knows himself by objectifying himself) and that he can achieve knowledge of the world (man is at home in the world insofar as he works on it, shaping it both intellectually and practically). Thus, in virtue of work, self-knowledge is seen to be a knowledge of an object, and knowledge of the world is seen to be knowledge of a human product.

(iii) In proclaiming the reconciliation of subject and object, Hegel is also subscribing to a form of *rationalism*. He is asserting that there are no irreducible mysteries, that everything is in principle capable of being comprehended by reason. This rationalism is a rejection alike of religious obscurantism and of philosophical scepticism — and we remember that, in the Introduction, a starting-point of the *Phenomenology* was the need to overcome a certain kind of scepticism. In part Hegel has attempted to vindicate his rationalism by attacking certain specific theories which postulate an 'unknowable' — as the Kantian thing-in-itself, or as the remote and unchanging 'beyond' of the Unhappy Consciousness. But he also appeals to a more general positive thesis: reason is capable of comprehending the world, because the world is in some sense constituted by reason. Hence —

(iv) Hegel's rationalism in turn rests on some kind of *idealism*, which is therefore a further meaning of the 'reconciliation of subject and object'. At this point, then, I want to take up again a question which has been discussed in previous chapters: In what sense is Hegel an idealist?

3. We could usefully begin by invoking Kant's distinction between *transcendental idealism* and *empirical idealism*. A representative of the latter is Berkeley, whose idealism amounts to the assertion that 'there are no material substances, but only ideas'. Empirical idealism, in other words, is a claim about what sorts of entity do and do not exist; a distinction is made between two sorts of entity, 'material substances' on the one hand and 'ideas' on the other, and it is then claimed that ideas do, material substances do not, exist. Transcendental idealism, on the other hand — by which phrase Kant refers to his own variety of idealism — does not involve any particular claim about what entities do or do not exist. Rather it is a 'higher level' or 'second order' idealism, a view of *what is involved* in any claims about the existence of this or that kind of entity. For the transcendental idealist, substances do exist, but what entitles us to assert this is the fact that 'substance' is itself one of the categories in terms of which we organize and order our experience. And it is because these categories are held to be what the mind itself contributes to experience that such a position is entitled to be called a form of 'idealism'. To put it another way, empirical idealism is a claim made *within* the categories of experience, whereas transcendental idealism is a claim about the *status* of those categories — the claim that

they are, so to speak, 'mind-made'.

In terms of this distinction, I would say that the principal and most fruitful strand in Hegel's idealism is a form of *transcendental* idealism. It is here that Hegel is closest to Kant. I have suggested previously that we can bring out the similarity between Hegel's enterprise and Kant's by seeing the *Phenomenology* as a 'deduction of the categories'. Moreover, Hegel would regard it not just as a process of discovering the categories but also as a demonstration that the categories are in fact 'mind-made'. This he takes to be shown by the very fact that, in the course of the *Phenomenology*, consciousness is able to generate all the categories out of itself and out of its own experience. At several points in the 'Preface', Hegel describes the development of the *Phenomenology* in the following terms. At each stage, he says, consciousness goes through a two-fold process of first objectifying itself and giving itself a content, and then criticising this content, negating and sublating it, turning it from a supposedly self-contained abstraction into a determinate moment having its place in the process as a whole. And, claims Hegel, this process — the ability of consciousness both to give itself a content and then to negate this content — is what guarantees that the content is not something alien and external but is itself the product of mind.

> 'The movement of being consists partly in becoming an 'other' and thus developing into its own immanent content; partly, again, it takes this content, this existence it assumes, back into itself, i.e. makes itself into a moment, and reduces itself to simple determinateness . . . . It is in this way that the content shows its specific characteristic not to be received from something else and stuck on externally; the content gives itself this determinate characteristic, appoints itself of its own initiative to the rank of a moment and to a place in the whole.' (p. 111).

We might recall too the emphasis in the Introduction on the fact that the development of the *Phenomenology* is entirely the work of consciousness; all that we have to do is look on. It is in the light of this that Hegel is now able to claim that the categories of experience made available by the *Phenomenology* are equally the work of consciousness.

This idealism is, as I have said, the basis of Hegel's rationalism. The world can be known and comprehended by reason because the world is, in this sense, *constituted* by reason. Nothing is in principle unknowable, since any supposed unknowable would itself have to be identified by means of the categories of rational thought, and thus would be characterised in some determinate way.

In saying this we are showing Hegel's idealism to be more thoroughgoing and, as he would claim, more consistent than Kant's. For, as I have repeatedly insisted, the Kantian thing-in-itself is just such an 'unknowable' as Hegel's idealism excludes. Its incompatibility with transcendental idealism is indeed evident even from Kant's own treatment of it in the *Critique of Pure Reason*. If the 'thing-in-itself' is defined as a reality which is prior to and independent of the categories, then Kant must go on to assert that *nothing whatsoever* can be said about it. This he does. But even in referring to it, in describing it as a 'thing-in-itself', he has contravened his own prescription. More specifically, his account of it seems to involve the employment of such categories as 'substance' and 'causality', 'unity' and 'plurality', 'reality', 'existence', etc.

Hegel, then, is a more consistent idealist than Kant. The difference between the two could be formulated as follows. Although I have suggested that Hegel is akin to Kant in being a *transcendental* idealist, he would not follow Kant in asserting his idealism to be a purely *formal* idealism. The suggestion that the categories determine only the 'form' of experience immediately invites talk of some independently specifiable 'matter' to which the categories are applied — and this then lets in the notion of 'things-in-themselves' as the 'reality' to be contrasted with the 'appearances' resulting from the imposition of the categories.[1] We have seen, especially in the section on 'Reason's Certainty and Reason's Truth', how strongly critical Hegel is of this distortion of idealism. He calls it a 'one-sided, unsound idealism', an 'abstract empty idealism' (cf. above, pp. 69-70). In later works he refers to it as 'subjective idealism', in contrast to his own 'absolute idealism'.[2]

Closely connected with all this is a further difference between Hegel and Kant. When Kant regards the categories as the work of the human mind, as imposed on experience by consciousness, he means the *individual* human mind, the *individual* consciousness. Certainly he would emphasise the universality of the categories, the fact that they are the same for different individuals, but he provides no adequate explanation of this. His account is framed in terms of each individual human mind applying the categories to its own sensory intake so as to constitute its own individual experience, and it just so happens that all human individuals apply the same categories — a consequence, perhaps, of the existence of a common human physiology. For Hegel, on the contrary, mind is inherently *social*. This is one of the most important insights to emerge from the *Phenomenology*. Insofar as the work reveals the identity of subject and object, this does not mean that Hegel assumes from the start a certain conception of the subject of consciousness and then proceeds to show that all the content of experience is reducible to states of this conscious subject. If the conception of the object undergoes development, so also does the conception of the subject. The *Phenomenology* begins, in 'Sense-certainty', with a view of the subject as a passive and isolated individual spectator. In due course this picture comes to be radically modified. It emerges that the subject is not just passive but also and primarily active, and that it is not merely individual but social. Thus the categories of human thought have to be seen as a *social* product. We might reasonably add, I think, especially on the strength of the 'Sense-certainty' section, that their social character is closely linked with their being encapsulated in *language*. It is the fact of being a social product that gives the categories their *objective* status — they are not just the private and personal creations of the individual consciousness. This, then, is a further respect in which Hegel can distinguish his own position from a 'subjective' idealism. For the individual, the categories are objectively given. But this does not mean that they are totally alien. Being social, they can be, for the individual, both objective yet also the products of the human mind. Only in a world where the individual is alienated from the social substance do they, in common with other social products, take on a reified appearance.

So far I have been presenting Hegel's idealism in what I would regard as a favourable light. I have been focusing on that strand in his thought which seems to me to constitute a plausible and indeed attractive form of idealism — a position which could be described as 'Kantianism, minus the thing-in-itself, plus a social theory of mind'. It has to be admitted, however, that there is another important strand in Hegel's idealism, and one which I regard as much less attractive. It can be introduced by looking again at the connection between Hegel's idealism and his rationalism. I have suggested that the former underpins the latter insofar as Hegel asserts that the world can be comprehended by reason because it is the work of reason. Now, I have taken the assertion that 'the world is the work of reason' to mean that anything can be an object of experience only insofar as it is brought under concepts and is therefore, in that sense, constituted by human thought. But there is also a much stronger sense which could be given to the assertion, so that Hegel would then be saying something like this: 'The world is created by God, it is the product of divine reason, and human minds can understand that world because the reason which they employ is identical with the divine reason'. And the notion of divine creation would be further elaborated by giving a stronger sense to the talk of mind 'objectifying itself'; the divine mind, it would be said, *creates* the world by *thinking* it. On this interpretation, then, Hegel's idealism would be a form of theism. It would be much closer to Berkeley's idealism than we have previously allowed. And we should have to understand Hegel's critique of religion as an objection not to religion as such but to an over-pictorialised religion. Hegel would have to be interpreted as some kind of pantheist (or, bearing in mind his explicit rejection of pantheism, as what has been called a 'panentheist'[3]).

This interpretation receives greater support from Hegel's later and posthumous works – for example, the two versions of the *Logic*, the *Lectures on the Philosophy of History*, and the *Lectures on the Philosophy of Religion* – where Hegel slips into religious language much more readily. But there is sufficient evidence for it in the *Phenomenology* to make plausible the claim that the difference is only one of emphasis. There can be no doubt that Hegel does sometimes, in the *Phenomenology*, verge on such a thesis. I do not think that he sufficiently distinguishes it from the form of idealism which I have previously been attributing to him. He fails to make the distinction, partly because the notion of 'mind' or 'spirit' remains in the end ambiguous; it is not clear whether 'spirit' transcends the individual mind simply in the sense of being social or in some much stronger sense which makes it akin to the traditional conception of God. And, as I have indicated, there is also a crucial ambiguity in the notion of objectification: does this denote simply the human activity of working on the world, shaping and forming it both in practice and by the application of language and concepts, and thereby rendering it a possible object of human comprehension? or does it also mean that the material world is in some sense a projection of divine thought? The following passages from the 'Preface' show how the latter interpretation cannot be excluded:

'The living substance . . . is that being which is truly subject, or, what is the same thing, is truly realized and actual solely in the process of positing itself, or in mediating with its own self its transitions from one state or position to the opposite . . . . The life of God and divine intelligence, then, can, if we like, be spoken of as love

113

disporting with itself. . . . That substance is essentially subject is expressed in the idea which represents the Absolute as spirit – the grandest conception of all, and one which is due to modern times and its religion. Spirit is alone reality. It is the essence or being-in-itself; it assumes determinate form and enters into relations with itself – it is other-being and being-for-itself; yet, in this determination, and in its otherness, it is still one with itself – it is in-and-for-itself.' (pp. 80-1, 85-6).

We have seen that Hegel uses this terminology to describe the development of the *Phenomenology*; each stage, each form of consciousness, is an objectification of spirit, which spirit then takes back into itself. But when, as here, Hegel goes further and suggests that reality itself is an objectification of spirit, and when he identifies this 'spirit' with 'God', he does seem committed to what I have referred to as the stronger and theistic form of idealism.

I am reluctant to attribute such a position to Hegel, because I regard it as a much less satisfactory form of idealism. If the *Phenomenology* is intended to establish it, it cannot be said to have successfully done so. Nor could such a position constitute any effective answer to scepticism. If, in order to establish rationalism and banish scepticism, we had to identify the reason at work in the world, compare it with human rationality and reveal the identity of the two, such a task could not be carried out. We cannot step outside our own rationality. The only proper answer to scepticism is to show that nothing could conceivably count as an independent comparison between reality on the one hand and our conceptual categories on the other, and that this whole model is misleading. The attempt to show this constitutes the successful side of the *Phenomenology*. But insofar as Hegel himself lapses into an acceptance of the misleading model, he is capitulating to precisely the kind of scepticism which he confronted in the 'Introduction'.

The same problem arises with Hegel's assertion that human *history* is the work of reason. On the one hand, this can be understood as the claim that history has a meaning, that it falls into a pattern and exhibits a coherent development, even though this meaning may not be apparent to or intended by the individual human agents who produce the events of history. On this view, the 'reason' in history is a product of, but is not reducible to, the reason of individuals in history. But Hegel also seems committed to a stronger thesis, that the reason operative in history is a supra-human reason, akin to a divine providence. Once again, the stronger thesis is more apparent in later works such as the *Lectures on the Philosophy of History,* but there are undeniable intimations of it in the *Phenomenology,* as for example in the following passage:

> 'Because the substance of the individual, nay, more, because the world-spirit has had the patience to go through these forms in the long stretch of time's extent, and to take upon itself the prodigious labour of world history, where it bodied forth in each form the entire content of itself, as each is capable of presenting it; and because by nothing less could it attain to consciousness of itself – for that reason, the individual mind, in the nature of the case, cannot by less toil grasp its own substance. All the same, its task has meanwhile been made much lighter, because this has been accomplished in itself.' (pp. 90-1).

If Hegel is here ascribing to the world-spirit an existence entirely independent of individual minds, this position may seem an extension of the previous one, but actually transforms it into its opposite. The strength of Hegel's philosophy of history lies in the recognition that history can have a rational meaning even though this meaning is not intended by any individual mind or minds. But Hegel then effectively denies this when he intimates that, because history reveals a rational development, it must be the work of a single *divine* mind.

This stronger thesis is connected with a further aspect of Hegel's idealism, which we looked at in chapter 5. The idea of history as the work of a divine mind encourages Hegel's tendency to treat history as the history of thought, the history of successive forms of consciousness. As we saw, this makes nonsense of the real nature of historical change. It leads Hegel to view historical changes simply as changes in consciousness; it makes for the illusion that human social life can be transformed merely by changes of attitude.

To sum up: when Hegel asserts that Absolute Knowledge involves the reconciliation of subject and object, he commits himself to some kind of philosophical idealism. I have been considering two versions of idealism which can be attributed to him. One is a form of 'transcendental idealism', but without the objectionable features of Kant's formulation of that doctrine. The other is a pantheistic view of reality as the emanation of a divine mind. And I have suggested that the former thesis is much more satisfactory than the latter.

In discussing Hegel's idealism, I have moved away from the direct consideration of the section on 'Absolute Knowledge'. I want now to return to that section by looking at the other main claim which Hegel makes about the nature of Absolute Knowledge.

4. In the Preface, the identity of subject and object is linked with the idea of philosophy as a *system*. The two ideas are in effect equated when Hegel says, for example:

> 'That the truth is only realized in the form of system, that substance is essentially subject, is expressed in the idea which represents the Absolute as Spirit . . . ' (p. 85).

Elsewhere in the Preface, the claim that philosophy must constitute a system is restated as the claim that it must become a *science*:

> 'The true shape in which truth exists can only be the scientific system. To help bring philosophy nearer to the form of science — that goal where it can lay aside the name of "love of knowledge" and be *actual knowledge* — that is what I have set before me.' (p. 70).

At first sight it is difficult to see the connection between the subject-object identity and the view of philosophy as a system. The connection is, however, clarified in the section on Absolute Knowledge. In the latter part of that section, Hegel explains that the sequence of forms of consciousness through which spirit has objectified itself can, when completed, be reformulated as a system of concepts.

> 'With absolute knowledge, then, spirit has wound up the process of its embodiment, so far as the assumption of those various forms is affected with the insurmountable distinction [between subject and object] which consciousness implies. Spirit has attained the pure element of its existence, the concept . . . . Seeing, then, that spirit has attained the concept, it unfolds its existence and develops its processes in this ether of its life and is *science*. The moments of its process are set forth therein no longer as determinate forms of consciousness, but — since the distinction which consciousness implies has gone back into the self — as determinate concepts and as the organic self-constituted process of these concepts.' (p. 805).

This scientific system of concepts is subsequently elaborated by Hegel in the *Logic,* the *Philosophy of Nature,* and the *Philosophy of Mind* (which together comprise the *Encyclopaedia of the Philosophical Sciences*). So the relation of the *Phenomenology* to the system is that of the 'process of discovery' to its result. Each form of consciousness in the *Phenomenology* has its own characteristic concepts, which are to be retained as elements in the total system, and the concepts can therefore initially be discovered by following the sequence of the *Phenomenology*. The same relation is specified in the Preface:

'. . . substance shows that it is in reality subject. When it has brought out this completely, mind has made its existence adequate to and one with its essential nature . . . . With the attainment of this the *Phenomenology of Mind* concludes. What mind prepares for itself in the course of its phenomenology is the element of true knowledge. In this element the moments of mind are now set out in the form of thought pure and simple, which knows its object to be itself. . . . The process by which they are developed into an organically connected whole is Logic or Speculative Philosophy.' (p. 97).

What Hegel understands by 'system' should be contrasted with what he is often taken to mean. Bertrand Russell offers us the following typical caricature:

'The view of Hegel . . . is that the character of any portion of the universe is so profoundly affected by its relations to the other parts and to the whole, that no true statement can be made about any part except to assign it its place in the whole. Since its place in the whole depends upon all the other parts, a true statement about its place in the whole will at the same time assign the place of every other part in the whole. Thus there can be only one true statement; there is no truth except the whole truth.' (Bertrand Russell: *A History of Western Philosophy* p. 770).

This passage represents a common misconception. Hegel's view of philosophy as a scientific system is taken to be a claim that all particular events are interconnected, and that any particular fact about the world can be logically deduced by reason alone. Hegel is understood as claiming to have systematised all human knowledge. This we can see to be a travesty of his position. His 'system' is in fact a system of *categories* — a framework of fundamental concepts in terms of which the world is to be comprehended. He regards them as forming a coherent and interconnected system in the sense that any one of them is fully intelligible only when considered in the context of its specific place within the system and of its relations to all the other concepts. In this sense, from any one concept, the rest can be deduced, for our attempt to

117

understand the application of one concept will require us to postulate others with which it is directly connected, and these in turn will lead to others, until the system is complete. Such a process is to be found in one form in the *Phenomenology,* and in another in the *Encyclopaedia.*

Nevertheless there are difficulties in Hegel's position, and the trouble is caused once again by his idealist view of history, his tendency to treat history simply as a development within consciousness, as a process of increasing knowledge. Interpreting the *Phenomenology* as the deduction of a system of categories makes good sense when applied to the early sections. One can defend the suggestion that the concepts belonging to the various stages of Consciousness – 'particular' and 'universal', 'thing' and 'property', 'force' and 'expression', 'appearance' and 'reality', etc. – are to be all retained as necessary moments in a total conceptual framework. There are objections to saying the same of Self-consciousness, as we saw in chapter 3. 'Recognition', 'work', 'discipline', etc. may indeed be necessary moments of Self-consciousness, but the roles of 'master' and 'slave', for example, are historically specific phenomena rather than universal elements in human experience. And this problem becomes acute when we turn to the second half of the *Phenomenology* and history comes to the fore. Presumably Hegel would again say that the modes of social life encountered in the historical stages of Spirit – 'the Family' and 'the Nation', 'State Power' and 'Wealth' – have to be preserved as moments in the totality. Accordingly we meet them again as 'the Family', 'Civil Society' and 'the State', the three main categories of ethical life specified in the *Philosophy of Mind* and in the *Philosophy of Right.* By this method, however, Hegel has transformed these historically specific institutions into timeless categories of social life. And we might wish to reply that, so far from being preserved as moments in a total system, they need to be historically superseded. The same goes for Hegel's treatment of religion. His method requires us to see it as a necessary element in human experience, and it re-appears as such in the *Philosophy of Mind.* And yet, following Hegel's own critique of religion in the *Phenomenology*, we might see good reason not for retaining religion as a moment in the 'system', but for discarding it.

These difficulties are highlighted in Hegel's use of the term 'aufheben'. In ordinary German the word is ambiguous in a way which, according to Hegel, makes it peculiarly appropriate for describing the relation between each stage and its successor in the *Phenomenology.* Discussing the transition from Sense-certainty to Perception, he says:

'The This, then, is established as *not this,* or as *superseded* (aufgeho-
ben), and yet not nothing, but a determinate nothing, *a nothing with
a content,* viz. *the This.* The sense-element is in this way itself still
present, not however in the form of some particular that is "meant",
as had to be the case in immediate certainty, but as a universal, as
that which will have the character of a *property. Cancelling, superseding* (Aufheben), reveals its true twofold meaning which we found
contained in the negative: it is at once *to negate* and *to preserve.'*
(p. 163f).

This can indeed be a fruitful ambiguity, drawing attention to the positive aspect of negation. In the absence, however, of any further elaboration of the precise way in which what is negated is also preserved, the
ambiguity is also a dangerous ambiguity. It is one thing to say that
sense-certainty's preoccupation with particulars, though false when
taken in abstraction, is valid as a moment of experience as a totality.
It is quite another thing to say that, because 'the Family' or 'the
State' are to be found at certain stages of history, the critical negation
of them must nevertheless preserve them as necessary features of social
life. The ambiguity of 'aufheben' here becomes a mere intellectual
sleight of hand, turning social contradictions into moments of an all-
embracing 'system'.

Ironically, the effect of the Hegelian procedure is to de-historicise
these social categories, and so to banish history from the philosophical
scene. I say 'ironically' because at a certain level Hegel is the philosopher least open to this charge. One of his main achievements is to have
brought history into the centre of philosophy. Unlike most of his predecessors he takes the history of philosophy seriously, viewing it not
as a sequence of mistakes but as the 'progressive evolution of the
truth' (p. 68) through a series of, in themselves, one-sided stages. He
also places philosophy in a wider historical perspective, insofar as he
relates the one-sidedness of particular forms of thought to social divisions − the individualism of epistemological or ethical theories is, for
example, related to the individualism of a 'self-estranged' society. There
remains, however, a crucial lack of clarity about the precise nature of
this relation, and this shows itself in his tendency to dissolve forms of
social life into forms of thought and so to eliminate real social conflicts.
5. The examination of Absolute Knowledge, and of Hegel's notion of
'system', helps to clarify two Hegelian concepts which we have previously left only half explained − those of 'necessity' and of the 'dialectic'.

When looking at the Introduction, we noted Hegel's claim that the transition from each stage of the *Phenomenology* to the next is in some sense a necessary one:

'The completeness of the forms of unreal consciousness will be brought about precisely through the necessity of the advance and the necessity of their connection with one another.' (p. 137).

If we then ask what kind of 'necessity' Hegel has in mind, an obvious possibility to consider is that he means 'logical necessity'. Since it is difficult, however, to see how the actual development of the *Phenomenology* could be regarded as a logically necessary progression, this had led some writers to suggest that Hegel is in fact concerned with something looser and less rigorous than logical necessity. J.N. Findlay is one such writer:

'In spite of anything [Hegel] may *say* regarding their necessary, scientific character, his transitions are only necessary and inevitable in the rather indefinite sense in which there is necessity and inevitability in a work of art . . . . At any point in the development, only *certain* continuations would seem natural and fitting. There is not, however, one continuation which alone seems obligatory, but rather a number of permissible continuations, some of which seem more fitting than others . . . . Hegel is, of course, wholly wrong if he thinks that the particular dialectical trail that he blazes is the *only* one that thought can follow: quite obviously his embarrassments could have been developed in different ways at every point . . . . The effort to see the wood for the arbitrary trees is, in the case of Hegel, often superhuman; it becomes easier when one realizes that the trees *are* disposed in an arbitrary manner.' (*Hegel: A Re-examination,* pp. 74 and 95. Cf. also pp. 109, 115 and 119).

There is a certain truth in these remarks; but as I shall try to show, they can also be profoundly misleading.

The first thing to be said is that the relations between the sections of the *Phenomenology* are not logical entailments, and this for the very simple reason that the relations in question are not primarily relations between propositions. This by itself is enough to dispose of the idea that the 'necessary' progression envisaged by Hegel is the deductive necessity of a Spinozistic system. The relations with which he is dealing are relations between *forms of consciousness,* and accordingly also relations between their respective *sets of concepts.*

The fact that such relations are not entailment-relations does not, however, mean that they are loose or unrigorous, let alone 'arbitrary'. If we wanted a single term with which to refer to them, we might perhaps use the term 'presupposition'. Each form of consciousness presupposes its successor − that is to say, in attempting to provide a coherent description of a certain form of consciousness we are logically required to postulate the existence of a different form of consciousness. There is nothing arbitrary about the connection. The relations between the various forms of consciousness are precise and specific relations − they are, in fact, the constitutive links of Hegel's 'system' which we have just been discussing.

What *can* be conceded to Findlay's position is that the stages of the *Phenomenology* do not have to be displayed in precisely that order. Whether Hegel actually thinks that the order of presentation is strict and unalterable, I am not sure, but he does not need to claim this. To use a rather banal analogy, Hegel's system can be likened to a jigsaw puzzle. Each piece has to fit into one particular position. It has to be precisely related to the other pieces. But there is no necessity for us to assemble the pieces in any particular order. Similarly Hegel could, from his discussion of Sense-certainty, have proceeded directly to the discussion of Self-consciousness, to the involvement of consciousness with action and work, or to the social dimension of consciousness, for Sense-certainty presupposes all of these, and Hegel's analysis could have been tailored to emphasise any one of these relations. The fact remains that these are necessary relations, as is, equally, the relation of Sense-certainty to Perception on which Hegel directly focuses. As a matter of strict logic, consciousness of sensory particulars involves the ability to employ universal terms referrring to the shared properties of objects − in short, such a consciousness necessarily presupposes a further kind of consciousness described by Hegel as Perception.

I should add that I do not regard all Hegel's transitions as equally *correct*. In some cases, certainly, the necessary relations which he claims to exhibit do not in fact exist. What I am arguing is that he does need to lay claim to this kind of necessity, that it is a strict necessity, and that the tendency to view the *Phenomenology* as a collection of useful but isolated insights can only make a mockery of it.[4]

As a further qualification, it once again has to be pointed out that the historical sections of the *Phenomenology* are less amenable to the interpretation I have offered. Indeed, the point has to be put more strongly: the notion of 'necessity' which I have attributed to Hegel could not possibly apply to a historical sequence. If the existence of stage A logically requires the existence of stage B, this is just to say that A and B cannot be separated in time, and so, *a fortiori,* B cannot be the historical successor to A. I do not think that one can consistently say what kind of necessity Hegel is dealing with in the second, historical, half of the *Phenomenology*. The necessity of a historical development is there presented as the necessity of a logical progression; in other words, the 'necessity' in question is a hybrid, neither one thing nor the other. As we shall now see, the same difficulty arises with Hegel's notion of 'dialectic'.

6. The 'dialectic' is the dynamic aspect of the 'system' and its 'necessity'. Since the various forms of consciousness and their respective concepts make up an interconnected system, the discussion of them in the *Phenomenology* is a constant and relentless movement from one form to another. A famous passage in the Preface connects these two aspects of Hegel's philosophy, the aspect of a static organised system and that of a dynamic dialectical process:

> 'It is the process that creates its own moments in its course, and goes through them all; and the whole of this movement constitutes its positive content and its truth . . . . Appearance is the process of coming into being and passing away again, a process that does not itself come into being and pass away, but exists in itself and constitutes the reality and the life-movement of truth. The truth is thus the bacchanalian revel, where not a member is sober; and because every member no sooner becomes detached than it *eo ipso* collapses straightway, the revel is just as much a state of transparent unbroken calm.' (p. 105).

The term 'dialectic' itself occurs very rarely in the *Phenomenology*[5]. This is revealing. It suggests that Hegel does not set out to propound a 'theory' of 'the dialectic'. Rather, he finds his philosophy naturally taking a certain form, and lights upon the word 'dialectical' as a suitable description of this form. The most informative general definition of 'dialectic' occurs in the section on Scepticism, where Hegel says:

> 'Dialectic as a negative process, taken immediately as it stands, appears to consciousness, in the first instance, as something at the mercy of which it is, and which does not exist through consciousness itself. In Scepticism, on the other hand, this negative process is a moment of self-consciousness . . . . By means of this self-conscious

negation, self-consciousness procures for itself the certainty of its own freedom . . . . What vanishes is what is determinate, the difference which, no matter what its nature or when it comes, sets up to be fixed and unchangeable. The difference has nothing permanent in it, and must vanish before thought because to be differentiated just means not to have being in itself, but to have its essential nature solely in other.' (pp. 247-8).

This description needs to be treated with caution, since the Sceptical attitude emphasises the negative side of dialectic at the expense of the positive. Nevertheless, with this reservation, the account tallies with Hegel's definition of 'dialectic' in the *Lesser Logic*:

'By Dialectic is meant the indwelling tendency outwards by which the one-sidedness and limitation of the predicates of understanding is seen in its true light, and shown to be the negation of them . . . . Thus understood the Dialectical principle constitutes the life and soul of scientific progress, the dynamic which alone gives immanent connexion and necessity to the body of science.' (*The Logic of Hegel*, p. 147).

Now, if the term 'dialectic' refers to the dynamic aspect of the system of concepts, the 'movement' which it indicates must be, not a literal movement in space and time, but a logical progression. It is a 'movement' only in the sense that, in tracing this logical progression, we are compelled to follow a succession of transitions from one concept to another, from 'particular' to 'universal' and so on. And the concepts in question are not just any concepts but the most general concepts, the essentially philosophical concepts which make up our basic categorial framework. Hegel is, of course, concerned above all with the traditional pairs of opposites such as 'subject' and 'object', 'particular' and 'universal', 'appearance' and 'reality'. When it is said that the dialectic breaks down the fixity of concepts, this means that the oppositions are not absolute, that each term involves and presupposes its opposite, in ways which we have experienced in the course of the *Phenomenology*.

That Hegel distinguishes philosophical concepts from other kinds of concepts appears to be confirmed by a passage in the Preface where he criticises philosophers who apply the thesis-antithesis-synthesis triad mechanically and indiscriminately to 'sense-determinations picked up from ordinary intuition' equally with 'pure determinations of thought, such as subject, object, substance, cause, universality, etc.' (p. 108.

Cf. pp. 116^{26}-117^7.). Similarly he distinguishes between the character of philosophical propositions and other sorts of propositions:

> 'Dogmatism as a way of thinking, in knowledge and in the study of philosophy, is nothing else but the view that truth consists in a proposition which is a fixed result, or again is immediately known. To questions like "When was Caesar born?", "How many feet make a furlong?", etc., a straight answer ought to be given; just as it is absolutely true that the square of the hypotenuse is equal to the sum of the squares of the other two sides of a right-angled triangle. But the nature of a so-called truth of that sort is different from the nature of philosophical truths.' (pp. 99-100).

In another passage later in the Preface (pp. 118-124), Hegel explicitly applies the concept of dialectic to the specific features of philosophical propositions. The discussion turns on the relation between subject and predicate in philosophical propositions. Hegel suggests that, whereas an ordinary proposition assumes a fixed subject and proceeds to apply this or that predicate to it, in philosophical propositions the subject/ predicate distinction breaks down. The subject, instead of constituting 'a permanent base on which to proceed', is absorbed into the predicate and thereby redefined. Hegel provides an example:

> '. . . In the proposition "God is Being", the predicate is "being"; it has substantive significance, and thus absorbs the subject within it. "Being" is meant to be here not predicate but the essence. Thereby, God seems to cease to be what he was when the proposition was put forward, viz. a fixed subject.' (p. 121).

Contrast this with Hegel's previous example of a non-philosophical proposition: if we ask 'When was Caesar born?' we assume that we know whom we mean by 'Caesar', and the assertion 'Caesar was born in 102 B.C.' does not alter this meaning. It seems, then, that for Hegel philosophical propositions are neither purely analytic nor purely synthetic. The proposition 'God is Being' is not, I take it, intended to be true simply in virtue of the definition of the term 'God'; it makes a substantive assertion about the nature of God, but in doing so, it alters our conception of God. And Hegel implies that this is because we cannot give a meaning to the term 'God', in its philosophical use, by associating it with some sensory image, but only by the way in which we use it in propositions. (Indeed, he goes on to suggest that it is dangerous to use the term 'God' in philosophical discourse just because it conjures up figurative associations, and that therefore it is better to stick to terms such as 'being', 'the one', 'subject', etc.)

A further example might explain Hegel's point more effectively. Consider Spinoza's procedure in his *Ethics*. He begins with definitions of terms such as 'God', 'substance', 'attribute' and 'mode', and then proceeds to deduce, from these definitions together with certain axioms, various conclusions about the nature of God, substance, etc. He apparently assumes, then, that these are 'fixed subjects', whose meaning can be settled at the outset, and which retain the same meaning when various characteristics are subsequently predicated of them. But in fact, notoriously, we do not understand the meaning of 'God', 'substance' etc. in Spinoza's philosophy until we have seen the conclusions he arrives at about them. The initial definition of 'substance', for example, links it with the Aristotelian conception of a substance as an individual thing bearing various properties, but when Spinoza goes on to argue that there can be only one substance, our conception of 'substance' changes as we see that it is in effect identical with reality as a whole. Our conception of 'mode' also changes accordingly, when we see that the 'substance'/'mode' relation is used to elucidate the relation between reality as a whole and individual objects. Hegel would regard this as typical of philosophical propositions, and as indicating not that Spinoza's particular definitions were defective but simply that the structure he gave to his philosophy was a misleading one. Spinoza models his arguments on what Hegel calls 'ratiocinative thinking', instead of recognising their dialectical nature.

Hegel's view of philosophical propositions, then, amounts to a further emphasis on that fluidity of concepts which constitutes the dialectic in general. I take it as further evidence that, for Hegel, the dialectic is primarily a feature of *concepts*. But we have to face the difficulty which has been a constant theme of this chapter: Hegel sees *historical* change as exhibiting the *same* kind of dialectical movement as this conceptual progression. He does so because ultimately, for Hegel, historical development *is* a conceptual progression. And, important though it is to *relate* philosophy to history, to *equate* historical change with a logical sequence of concepts is to abolish the real movement of history.

This is the genesis of the Marxist reaction to Hegel. Engels puts it succinctly:

'According to Hegel, dialectics is the self-development of the concept . . . . The dialectical development apparent in nature and history, that is, the causal interconnection of the progressive movement from the lower to the higher, which asserts itself through all zigzag movements and temporary retrogressions, is only a copy of the self-movement of the concept going on from eternity, no one knows where, but at all events independently of any thinking human brain.' (*Ludwig Feuerbach and the End of Classical German Philosophy* pp. 386-7).

Engels' response is then to retain the idea of dialectic, but to treat it as a thesis about change in the physical world, in natural processes and in human history. In so doing, however, Engels makes the same mistake as Hegel, in a converse form. Hegel's mistake was to assimilate material and historical change to a conceptual progression. Instead of separating the one from the other, Engels, guided by Marx's phrase in the Preface to *Capital* about 'standing the dialectic on its feet',[6] simply assimilates the dialectic of concepts to material change. He says of himself and Marx:

'We comprehended the concepts in our heads once more materialistically — as images of real things instead of regarding the real things as images of this or that stage of the absolute concept. Thus dialectics reduced itself to the science of the general laws of motion, both of the external world and of human thought — two sets of laws which are identical in substance, but differ in their expression in so far as the human mind can apply them consciously, while in nature and also up to now for the most part in human history, these laws assert themselves unconsciously, in the form of external necessity, in the midst of an endless series of seeming accidents. Thereby the dialectic of concepts itself became merely the conscious reflex of the dialectical motion of the real world and thus the dialectic of Hegel was placed upon its head; or rather, turned off its head, on which it was standing, and placed upon its feet.' (*Ludwig Feuerbach* p. 387).

Engels' materialising of the dialectic is here assisted by his crude psychologising of logic. He interprets statements about the logical relations between concepts as statements about what goes on in people's minds when the employ those concepts, and then, on the basis of an equally crude materialist theory of mind, interprets these in turn as statements about the physical processes in people's brains. This whole approach is fallacious: in asserting a logical connection between concept A and concept B I am by no means asserting that whenever anyone thinks of A he also thinks of B.

The proper response to Hegel, then, would be to separate the two sides of the dialectic. Hegel's conceptual dialectic is valid and important in its own right, and certainly has nothing to do with any thesis about human brain-processes. The interconnections explored by Hegel between antithetical concepts, such as the dialectical movement from 'particular' to 'universal', are of great philosophical significance. Moreover, the 'laws of dialectic' which Engels formalises as principles of material change are most at home in this conceptual dialectic. The 'Law of the Interpenetration of Opposites' is best understood as referring to the conceptual interconnections already mentioned. The interpenetration of 'particular' and 'universal' is in fact instanced by Lenin as a classic example of the dialectic:

> 'To begin with what is the simplest, most common, etc., with *any proposition*: The leaves of a tree are green; John is a man; Fido is a dog, etc. Here already we have *dialectics* (as Hegel's genius recognized): the *individual is* the *universal* . . . . Consequently, the opposites (the individual is opposed to the universal) are identical: the individual exists only in the connection that leads to the universal. The universal exists only in the individual and through the individual. Every individual is (in one way or another) a universal . . . . Thus in *any* proposition we can (and must) disclose . . . *all* the elements of dialectics, and thereby show that dialectics is a property of all human knowledge in general'.
>
> (Lenin: 'On the Question of Dialectics', in *Philosophical Notebooks* p. 361).

Any attempt to 'materialise' this example would reduce it to absurdity. The point is not that particulars *turn into* universals through a process of physical change, but that, in virtue of the logical transition from the one concept to the other, particulars *are* universals. Similarly Engels' 'Law of the Negation of the Negation' (which would be better named 'the Law of Determinate Negation') is best understood as referring to the nature of conceptual transitions — we have seen that 'determinate negation' is the motive force behind the development of the *Phenomenology*. The 'law of the Transformation of Quantitative into Qualitative Change' is a more complicated case. It refers to the nature of *material* change, but what it draws attention to is the conceptual relation between 'quantity' and 'quality'. A quantitative change, when it reaches a certain point, *is also* a qualitative change, without thereby ceasing to be still a quantitative change. The opposed concepts 'quantity' and 'quality' interpenetrate, and this 'law' is really a subordinate case of the first law.

In arguing for the recognition of an independent *conceptual dialectic* and resisting the attempt to materialise it, I am not committed to any Platonic dualism of a world of concepts set apart from the material world. The conceptual dialectic does not consist in statements about concepts *as distinct from* statements about the physical world. It is true of particulars *in the physical world* that they can only be identified as particulars insofar as they are instantiations of universals. But this is a *conceptual* truth about particular entities in the world, rather than an empirical truth. It is discovered not by an empirical examination of particulars, but by examining the logical relations between the terms 'particular' and 'universal'. Thus the dichotomy which I *am* committed to is some kind of empirical/*a priori* dichotomy (thought I would add, in cryptic dialectical fashion, that this is not an absolute dichotomy).

What, then, can be said about the empirical dialectic if it is separated from the conceptual dialectic? It is in danger of becoming something rather banal, an assertion that 'there is change in the material world' — which will be news to no one. The thesis that 'concepts change into one another' is a challenging and important insight; the statement that 'things change into one another' is in itself a rather boring and obvious remark. No one apart from Parmenides and the Eleatics would ever have wanted to disagree with it and to assert that the universe is totally static. The emphasis on change in the material world does, however, become significant when it is applied to particular cases, when it is shown that what is commonly supposed to be static is actually something changing. Engels regularly invokes certain examples: the view of modern physics that the universe is to be comprehended fundamentally as a complex of processes rather than of things; the recognition that our solar system is not a set of unchanging planetary movements but arose out of an original nebular mass; the Darwinian theory of evolution, replacing the conception of a timeless classification of plant and animal species; and, above all, the recognition that social institutions, such as wage labour, capital, the family, the state, are historically specific institutions which arose in a particular social context and can likewise disappear.

These theses are all true and important. But they are also quite independent of one another. In particular, the fourth of them is an essential element of Marxism, whereas the other three are entirely independent of it. It can therefore be misleading to lump them all together under the single heading 'dialectic' if we thereby give the impression that they stand or fall together. In Hegel's case there would be some justification for this. To the extent that he sees changes in the physical world, and particularly historical changes, as the expression of the dialectical progression of concepts, he is entitled to bring them all under the label of 'the dialectic'. Engels, on the other hand, has correctly seen that the nature of changes in the physical world has to be determined empirically; he should therefore go on to recognise that different kinds of change have to be empirically discovered quite separately, and that there is no general, high-level law called 'the dialectic' of which they all serve as confirmations.

The appropriate use of the term 'dialectic', applied to change in the material world, would be not to refer to some single very general thesis, but rather to designate a certain mode of explanation, *developmental* explanation, and to emphasise the importance of such explanations. A situation which defies understanding when viewed simply in terms of its present state may become intelligible when seen as the product of a past development. The intellectual breakthrough achieved by Darwin, for example, was to show that the apparent purposive adaptation in living organisms can be understood by postulating a past development involving random genetic mutations, the inheritance of these mutant characteristics and the elimination of less successfully adapted organisms. Moreover, in order to understand a present situation we may need to consider not only its past development but also its future potentialities. The Marxist claim, for example, is that the proper understanding of capitalist society involves an understanding both of its development out of a previous form of society and of the direction in which the various forces within it are tending.

The notion of an empirical 'dialectic', then, can valuably be employed to refer not to a super-scientific law but to a particular mode of explanation. It can also serve to point out — and here we are led back to Hegel — the contrast between developmental explanation and the static mode of thought encouraged by the subject-predicate propositional form. Any change has to be described by means of propositions of the form 'Such-and-such an entity changes in such-and-such ways'. An account of the development of capitalist society, for example, naturally takes the form 'Capitalist society undergoes this or that change'. As Hegel has indicated, this form of expression implies the existence of a fixed subject, 'capitalist society', which persists throughout the changes. It may therefore blind us to the fact that the changes undergone by capitalist society may turn it into something *other than* capitalist society, so that the fixed subject in fact ceases to exist. This is true quite generally. Any change can be described only by predicating it of something which is itself supposed not to change. This may be a feature of language in general, or it may be a particular feature of certain languages, or, as Kant claims in the first Analogy of Experience, it may be a necessary feature of any conceptual scheme. That is a question which we cannot discuss here. But at any rate, the point is that this way of describing change tends to limit our perception of change. In making us aware of this, and of the general importance of change and development, Hegel contributed decisively to the notion of an empirical dialectic.

7. I have been emphasising Hegel's failure to distinguish sufficiently clearly between logical progression and historical change. I have also stressed, however, that it is his positive achievement to have connected epistemological and logical considerations with historical considerations, and I want to conclude by re-stating the nature of this achievement. Its positive and its negative aspects can be stated thus: history has a logic, and logic has a history — these are the great insights of the *Phenomenology*; but history and logic do not simply coincide — and therein lies the flaw of the *Phenomenology*.

History has a logic. That is to say, the development of human social life and social institutions exhibits a rational pattern. It is not an arbitrary sequence of unrelated incidents. We have seen that for Hegel history is a dialectic of particular and universal, of individual and society. Its first step is the emergence of the individual, the emancipation of the individual from a complete identification with social norms and customs. The isolated and separate individual, however, is then related to social products and institutions as alien entities set over against him. The completion of this historical process therefore requires that the individual come to recognise himself in these social products, it requires that he be reconciled with this social reality without thereby simply being reabsorbed into it.

Now to say that, in this sense, history has a logic is not to say that its development is explicable in terms of the logical relations between concepts. We have found that Hegel does in fact move too readily from the first claim to the second. He appears to suppose that, *in virtue of* the dialectical relation between 'particular' and 'universal', a society dominated by universal custom *must* give way to a society of separate and particularised individuals. He implies that the movement from the Ethical World to the Self-estranged World can be understood in the same kind of way as the movement from Sense-certainty to Perception. Again, in his discussion of the Self-estranged World he seems to suggest that, *because of* the dialectical interconnection of 'being-in-itself' and 'being-for-itself', a society in which the being-in-itself of consciousness is recognised and confirmed *must* develop in such a way that consciousness comes to assert also its being-for-itself. This assimilation, by Hegel, of historical change to logical relations must be rejected. There nevertheless remains a view of the logic of history which is important in its own right.

If history has a logic, so also logic has a history. Logic in Hegel's sense — the system of categories which structure human knowledge — can come to be known only through a process of historical development. This is stated explicitly at the end of the *Phenomenology*:

'. . . science does not appear in time and in reality till spirit has arrived at this stage of being conscious regarding itself.' (p.798)

And again:

'. . . until and unless spirit inherently completes itself, completes itself as a world-spirit, it cannot reach its completion as self-conscious spirit.' (p.801)

Only with the completion of history does absolute knowledge become possible. And with this must go the claim by Hegel that he himself stands at the end of history and has attained to absolute knowledge.

The claim is bound to appear a grandiose one. Nevertheless, if we avoid misunderstandings of the terms in which it is formulated — if we recognise that 'absolute knowledge' is not the accumulated knowledge of all possible facts about particular situations and states of affairs, and that 'the end of history' does not mean the cessation of all human achievement and change — then the claim is one which can be taken seriously. Given Hegel's conception of history, 'the end of history' must mean the stage of human development at which social institutions cease to have an alien existence and to react upon men with an apparent momentum of their own, but are recognised to be amenable to rational comprehension and rational control. This is the completion of history also in the sense that all the possible fundamental relations between the human subject and the objective world — absorption, alienation, and reconciliation — have now been experienced. It does not mean the inauguration of a completely static universe; rather, it means that 'history' now ceases to have any independent existence and henceforth simply coincides with the fully conscious activity of human reason. It is in this sense that the end of history makes possible absolute knowledge. Only now can reason become aware of its own nature and know itself to be all reality. In effect, 'the end of history' is the overcoming of alienation in the political and economic realm; 'absolute knowledge' is the overcoming of alienation in the epistemological realm; and the former is a precondition of the latter.[7]

In rendering plausible the idea of an 'end of history' we must remember too that this is not something which is achieved instantaneously. As Hegel says, although 'the sunrise, . . . in a flash and at a single stroke, brings to view the form and structure of the new world', nevertheless

'. . . this new world is perfectly realised just as little as the new-born child. . . . A building is not finished when its foundation is laid. . . . In the same way science, the crowning glory of a spiritual world, is not found complete in its initial stages.' (pp.75-6)

Though social institutions lose their alienated appearance and are recognised to be the objectification of human action, there still remains, in practice, the task of making them fully conform to reason. Though the structure of human concepts is recognised to be also the rational structure of the objective world, there still remains the theoretical task of articulating the precise character of this system of categories. As in Hegel's day, so in our own, both tasks wait to be completed.

[1] In the *Critique of Pure Reason*, Kant's use of the 'form/matter' dichotomy is especially prominent at the beginning of the 'Transcendental Aesthetic'. For his employment of the contrasts between 'transcendental' and 'empirical' idealism and between 'formal' and 'material idealism' see also, for example, the 'Refutation of Idealism', and 'The Antinomy of Pure Reason' section VI ('Transcendental Idealism as the Key to the Solution of Cosmological Dialectic').

[2] 'According to Kant, the things that we know about are *to us* appearances only, and we can never know their essential nature, which belongs to another world we cannot approach. Plain minds have not unreasonably taken objection to this subjective idealism, with its

reduction of the facts of consciousness to a purely personal world, created by ourselves alone. For the true statement of the case is rather as follows. The things of which we have direct consciousness are mere phenomena, not for us, only, but in their own nature. . . . This view of things, it is true, is as idealist as Kant's; but in contra-distinction to the subjective idealism of the Critical Philosophy should be termed absolute idealism.' (*The Logic of Hegel* pp.93f.)

[3] *Cf.* Robert C. Whittemore: 'Hegel as Panentheist', in *Tulane Studies in Philosophy* Vol. IX (1960).

[4] This tendency is further exhibited in the chapter on the *Phenome-nology* in Walter Kaufmann's *Hegel*.

[5] The only occurrences I can find are on pp. 123-4, 142, and 247-8. Of the ten occurrences on these pages, four link the word 'dialectic(al)' with the word 'movement', three with the word 'process', and one with the word 'restlessness'.

[6] Karl Marx: *Capital* Vol. I, pp. 19-20.

[7] It will be apparent that my interpretation of Hegel's 'end of history' brings it close to Marx's notion of the 'end of prehistory'.

The following works are referred to in the text.

H. B. Acton: *Kant's Moral Philosophy*, London, 1970

A. J. Ayer: *Language, Truth and Logic*, London, 1946

F. H. Bradley: *Ethical Studies*, Oxford, 1962

R. Descartes: *The Philosophical Works of Descartes*, translated by
    Haldane and Ross, Cambridge, 1911

K. R. Dove: 'Hegel's Phenomenological Method', in *New Studies in
    Hegel's Philosophy*, ed. W. E. Steinkraus, New York, 1971

F. Engels: *Ludwig Feuerbach and the End of Classical German
    Philosophy*, in Marx and Engels: *Selected Works*, Moscow, 1962

L. Feuerbach: *Critique of Hegel's Philosophy*, in *The Fiery Brook*:
    Selected Writings of Ludwig Feuerbach, translated by Zawar Hanfi,
    New York, 1972

J. N. Findlay: *Hegel – a Re-examination*, London, 1958

G. W. F. Hegel: *Lectures on the History of Philosophy*, translated by
    E. S. Haldane, London, 1892

G. W. F. Hegel: *The Logic of Hegel*, translated from the Encyclopaedia
    of the Philosophical Sciences by William Wallace, Oxford, 1892

G. W. F. Hegel: *On Art, Religion and Philosophy*, edited by J. Glenn
    Gray, New York, 1970

G. W. F. Hegel: *The Phenomenology of Mind*, translated by J. B. Baillie,
    London, 1931

G. W. F. Hegel: *The Philosophy of Hegel*, ed. C. J. Friedrich, New York,
    1953

G. W. F. Hegel: *The Philosophy of History*, translated by J. Sibree, New
    York, 1956

G. W. F. Hegel: *The Philosophy of Mind*, translated from the Encyclo-
    paedia of the Philosophical Sciences by William Wallace and A. V.
    Miller, Oxford, 1971

G. W. F. Hegel: *The Philosophy of Right*, translated by T. M. Knox,
    Oxford, 1952

D. Hume: *A Treatise of Human Nature*

I. Kant: *Critique of Practical Reason*

I. Kant: *Critique of Pure Reason*, translated by N. Kemp Smith, London,
    1933

W. Kaufmann: *Hegel*, London, 1968

R. D. Laing: *The Divided Self*, Harmondsworth, 1965

Bibliography

R. D. Laing: *Self and Others*, Harmondsworth, 1971

R. D. Laing and A. Esterson: *Sanity, Madness and the Family*, Harmondsworth, 1970

V. I. Lenin: *Collected Works Vol. 38: Philosophical Notebooks*, London and Moscow, 1961

J. Locke: *An Essay Concerning Human Understanding*

J. Loewenberg: 'The Comedy of Immediacy in Hegel's "Phenomenology" ' (in *Mind* 1935)

A. MacIntyre: *A Short History of Ethics*, London, 1967

J. Maier: *On Hegel's Critique of Kant*, New York, 1939

K. Marx: *Capital*, London, 1970

K. Marx: *Economic and Philosophical Manuscripts*, in *Early Writings* translated by T. B. Bottomore, London, 1963

M. Merleau-Ponty: *The Phenomenology of Perception*, translated by C. Smith, London, 1962

B. Russell: *A History of Western Philosophy*, London, 1946

B. Russell: *Mysticism and Logic*, London, 1917

J-P. Sartre: *Being and Nothingness*, translated by Hazel E. Barnes, London, 1957

M. G. Singer: *Generalization in Ethics*, London, 1963

Sophocles: *The Theban Plays*, translated by E. F. Watling, Harmondsworth, 1947

W. H. Walsh: *Hegelian Ethics*, London, 1969

G. J. Warnock: *Berkeley*, Harmondsworth, 1969

R. C. Whittemore: 'Hegel as Panentheist', in *Tulane Studies in Philosophy* Vol. IX, 1960

L. Wittgenstein: *Philosophical Investigations*, Oxford, 1953

INDEX

Entries within inverted commas refer to sections of the *Phenomenology of Mind*.

137

system, 116-9

things-in-themselves, 10-11, 17, 22, 40, 69, 108, 109, 111
totality, 43f

'Unhappy Consciousness, The', 59-64, 95f, 108, 109
universal and particular, 26, 29-38, 118, 127, 130

universalisability, 78-80

Walsh, W. H., 85
Warnock, G. J., 33, 45
wealth, 89-94, 99, 118
Whittemore, R. C., 133
Wittgenstein, L., 14, 27, 84
work, 44, 50, 52-6, 61f, 64, 72f, 108, 118